D1356026

WHAT THE CEO *REALLY* WANTS FROM YOU

WHAT THE CEO *REALLY* WANTS FROM YOU

THE 4 As FOR MANAGERIAL SUCCESS

R. GOPALAKRISHNAN

With Forewords by

PAUL POLMAN, RAM CHARAN AND
SHANTANU NARAYEN

COLLINS BUSINESS
An Imprint of HarperCollins Publishers

First published in India in 2012 by Collins Business
An imprint of HarperCollins *Publishers* India
a joint venture with
The India Today Group

HarperCollins *Publishers*
A-53, Sector 57, Noida, Uttar Pradesh 201301, India
77-85 Fulham Palace Road, London W6 8JB, United Kingdom
Hazelton Lanes, 55 Avenue Road, Suite 2900, Toronto, Ontario M5R 3L2
and 1995 Markham Road, Scarborough, Ontario M1B 5M8, Canada
25 Ryde Road, Pymble, Sydney, NSW 2073, Australia
31 View Road, Glenfield, Auckland 10, New Zealand
10 East 53rd Street, New York NY 10022, USA

Typeset in 12/16 Requiem Regular at
SŪRYA

Printed and bound at
Thomson Press (India) Ltd.

I dedicate this book to the many subordinates, peers and bosses with whom I have worked for over forty-five years.

I thank all of them because they forgave my faults as a co-worker and gave me a chance to learn from my mistakes, which is why I have written this book.

I injured some, but since I could not repair the injuries I had done, I have tried to make amends by benefiting others.

—W. Somerset Maugham,
A Writer's Notebook

CONTENTS

ACCOMPLISHMENT

AFFABILITY

ADVOCACY

AUTHENTICITY

Negotiating an Ambiguous Environment

The world is changing at a faster rate than I can remember at any stage during my thirty-odd years in business. Power is shifting steadily—but inexorably—from west to east. Digitization is transforming the way we work and putting power directly into the hands of ordinary citizens. Our current form of capitalism is under question by many and the environment is under threat. Never has the need for leadership been greater.

The implications of these changes for business are profound. The world of work my three sons are entering today is almost unrecognizable from the one I knew at their age. Navigating the intricacies of this highly complex and interdependent world is no easy task. Unfortunately, there are no rule books. The old certainties have gone forever. As I frequently tell my Unilever colleagues, those who succeed in this environment will be those who learn to live with ambiguity. But also those who understand the power of collaboration better than others. The challenges are simply too big to undertake alone.

Partnerships with others, but above all with your direct boss and organization, are more important than ever before.

The term over-ambitious simply does not apply when you look at the scale of the challenges we have to solve in this current era. There is a fundamental readjustment going on as a result of the financial crisis, with a move from a rules-based society back to a principle- and values-led society. In this environment, cooperation is more important than ever.

'Living with ambiguity' would have been an equally appropriate title for this book. At its heart is the need for today's manager to constantly change and adapt in response to fast-moving events. However, unlike the plethora of books on how to be a better leader in this kind of environment, the focus of this work is on how to be better led. As such it provides a refreshing and distinctive approach. It explores the many ways in which to build that essential foundation of trust between leaders and managers—from more open conversations to the need for greater self-awareness. In this increasingly interdependent world, relationships and EQ are vitally important. So is the need to be driven by our internal compass, based on deep values and strong beliefs. I have certainly benefited during my career most when working the 4 As, so eloquently described by Gopal, and above all when my direct bosses understood them as well .

The strength of this book, in my view, also comes from two other factors.

First, the authority and experience of its author. Few people can lay claim to the career of R. Gopalakrishnan. The impact of his more than thirty years at Unilever is still felt today, more than fourteen years after he left. HUL, an admired institution for leadership development, would not have been what it is today without the passion for people and organization that Gopal championed throughout his career. He is a business heavyweight in every sense of the word and the benefit of his wisdom and experience shines through on every page.

Second, the guidance offered in this book is brilliantly illustrated and supplemented through a series of case studies. This is not some theoretical or abstract tome. As you would expect of a businessman of more than forty years standing, it is an immensely practical work, rooted in many real life examples for us to follow.

I am delighted to recommend this book and honoured to be asked to contribute a foreword. As Gopal rightly suggests, 'a career is a journey of constant and continuous learning'. Wherever you happen to be on the journey, this book will help to guide the way.

London
12 June 2012

PAUL POLMAN,
Chief Executive Officer, Unilever

ADOPTING A DISTINCTIVE APPROACH

I have known Gopal off and on for several years from his Unilever days. I am very happy to provide a few words as a perspective foreword to a remarkable book by Gopal. It is important for the development of any profession that experienced practitioners share their views with future practitioners—and that is exactly what Gopal has set out to do. All managers do not write and neither are all writers, good managers. Gopal combines both skills and so this book is special.

In 2000, I wrote a slim volume, *What the CEO Wants You to Know*, aimed at the rational, logical part of the brain. The book outlined in jargon-free language the basics of what business and commerce are all about. I stated that managers need to carry business knowledge in its simplest form, common sense, into solving complex business problems. I had argued that the task of a good leader is to simplify complexity, which is the packaging in which all business problems come dressed.

Gopal's book seems to address another side of the same coin. It is aimed at the emotional part of the brain. It is a distinctive and different approach. Each of us has a world view, an outlook and a mindset which shapes the way we view issues. For sure the world of the manager is influenced by the rational as well as the emotional parts of the brain.

When it comes to soft subjects like boss-subordinate relationships and obligations to the company, upcoming managers tend to view them from their background and perspective. Almost always they think more deeply about what the boss and company owes them, and more lightly, about what they owe in return. Upcoming managers read articles and books about leadership (I hope they do!) and subconsciously emulate the behavioural practices of people who have already become iconic leaders. Force fitting their work environment and behaviour into their preconceived mental models regrettably scuttles many a promising career.

Consider the story of Paul Richards narrated by me in my book *What the CEO Wants You to Know*.

Paul started as a salesman in a $5 billion company. He was remarkably successful in his assignments and was rapidly promoted until he came to head Europe. His CEO was visibly impressed and asked him to move to another division, whose business and industry were both unfamiliar to Paul. The division was failing to meet its targets.

Paul drove right in but struggled from the first day. He just could not unlearn his past industry knowledge, and relearn the knowledge required for this new industry. Paul faced a dilemma. On the one hand, Paul was happy that he took on the challenge offered by his CEO to demonstrate success in a new industry domain. It would positively influence the chances of his becoming company CEO in due course. On the other hand, he had to admit to himself that he could not adjust, that his chances of becoming CEO were diminishing by the day and, above all, he was unhappy. He then did what was right for the company and himself. He switched to another company in the industry domain he knew. When I met him, he told me that he felt 'liberated'.

Gopal argues that the 4 As are to be learned along the way on one's career and deployed in varying proportions as one climbs the corporate ladder: Accomplishment, Affability, Advocacy and Authenticity. The choice of these four attributes reflects the high importance given by him to human relationships in the development of a business career.

He is right.

I am delighted that Gopal has adopted an anecdotal style of narrating his experiences; it makes the book readable, not just once but again and again. I feel sure that the reader can benefit a great deal from Gopal's work for four and a half decades for India's most Indian multinational company, Unilever, as well as Tata, which is India's most multinational Indian company.

Dallas, Texas, USA   RAM CHARAN
10 June 2012   CEO and Board Advisor and
Best Selling Author

BUILDING A WINNING CAREER

I remember having a conversation years ago with Gopal, in Hawaii, over a glass of wine. My pending transition into the role of CEO was weighing heavily on my mind. Gopal helped me realize that even though I had been Chief Operating Officer—only one step away from the top job—becoming a CEO would change my perspectives and expectations of myself, my team, and my organization. His insights into the challenges of executive leadership clarified how I should approach my own role. I am thrilled that he is now sharing his wisdom with everyone who picks up this book.

Many management books outline what it takes for you to be a great leader once you have arrived. In reality, few of us spend the majority of our careers at the top. In *What the CEO Really Wants from You*, Gopal provides a refreshing perspective on how winning careers are built on great relationships between a rising leader and his or her boss; it focuses on what the CEO truly cares about—qualities that contribute to the company's overall success—and how they ultimately lead to career success.

My own journey did not follow an obvious path. Despite my MBA and passion for product development my progression was not always an upward path of ever-expanding responsibilities and scope. In fact, I was once asked by my CEO to take on a role that was narrower in scope and smaller in size organizationally. However, this seemingly less important role was strategically critical and was what my bosses needed from me. In hindsight, it was essential for my development— I learned about an emerging technology, developed deeper customer relationships, and undertook some difficult strategic and product decisions that affected people's jobs. The entire experience prepared me for what came next, and helped me become a better leader.

Today, as a CEO, I look at the many young executives and rising stars I have had the pleasure of working with and mentoring over the years. What has consistently set them apart from the other equally intelligent and hard-working employees is their ability to listen and understand different perspectives, to connect with people across departments and at all levels, to influence and mobilize virtual teams, to put the company's interests ahead of their departmental interests, and to be trusted to make decisions in a manner that is consistent with our company values. In many ways, they demonstrate Gopal's 4 straight As—Accomplishment, Affability, Advocacy, and Authenticity. I'm confident these individuals will go far.

We are never done learning, wherever we are in our careers. My own bosses, the co-founders and co-chairmen of Adobe, John Warnock and Chuck Geschke, have often told me that everyone has to reinvent themselves every few years. Reading Gopal's book—with sound theories made accessible through real-world anecdotes—has given me new insights to consider in my continuing journey as CEO in one of the most transformative times in the history of technology and business.

While Gopal has an incredible track record as a leader, in his heart he remains both a student of human behaviour as well as a teacher who loves to share his insights with those around him. I feel fortunate to have the opportunity to write this foreword and I hope every reader gets as much out of this book as I have.

California, USA   SHANTANU NARAYEN
29 June 2012   President & CEO,
                                            Adobe Systems

PREFACE

'I here present you with a few suggestions . . . little more than glimmerings . . . If I am addressing one of that numerous class, who read to be told what to think, let me advise you to meddle with this book no further . . . But if you are building up your opinions for yourself, and only want to be provided with the materials, you may meet with many things in these pages to suit you.'

—Julius Hare, English theologian,
(mid 1800s)

Many believe that attention spans have come down and that the days of McDonaldization are here to stay; that a management book has to be an easy-to-read 'how to' book which offers breathlessly urgent tips on becoming successful. There are others who do not believe this to be true.

My own experience is that managers, being a thinking lot, would love to have ideas and experiences thrown at them. They are used to the case study methodology, where they learn to debate the context and possible approaches. They are a far smarter lot these days compared to earlier generations. They have a huge absorptive capacity and they reflect on what touches them—in their own way.

What the CEO Really Wants from You attempts to leverage that capability.

The quotation by Julius Hare represents what went on in my mind throughout the time it took me to conceptualize and write this book. Did I have a new theory to offer? Did I have something to say which would be unique? Well, yes and no, depending on how you see it, but for sure, I do have something distinctive and practical to say.

The management world is replete with articles and books on how to succeed, how to get to the corner office fast and how to be a great leader. But the literature is thinner on how to be a great subordinate, how to deserve before desiring, and how to regard understanding what your boss needs as an integral part of your job. And if you have not been a great subordinate, you are not quite headed towards the C-suite or the corner office!

The idea of this book arose from trying to fill this gap. It is based on my experiences, observations and reflections over four decades in management and leadership. I have made so many errors of judgment throughout my career that it is an enduring surprise that I survived all of those.

I must thank my subordinates, peers and bosses over the last forty-five years for indulging me and by letting me learn lessons from my mistakes. Though my own experiences have been in industrial organizations, I have little doubt that the learnings and wisdom I have gleaned are applicable more generally. I have had the privilege to be a participant and an interlocutor over all these years.

When it comes to learning about leadership, we attend advanced courses, listen to gurus and read stories and books about successful leadership. A number of books, videos, courses and lectures are available on the subject of how to become a successful leader.

When it comes to human relationships, there are just a handful of truths and nuggets of wisdom in the world. These nuggets are part of storytelling and folklore in every society. People make nearly the same mistakes century after century.

How and where can you learn lessons about being a good subordinate? This book carries some relevant thoughts. The real challenge is not the technical part of completing the job. The challenge is to find the 'correct' pathway to adopt two apparently opposite requirements. For example:

- Get the job done on time *and* do not upset people.
- Speak the truth if you disagree *and* do not offend the boss.
- Keep your eyes and ears open in the company *and* do not gossip.
- Set ambitious goals *and* deliver on your targets.
- Be experimental *and* be consistent.

The key idea is that there is a middle path between such extremes. It is a bit like the two threatening monsters, Scylla and Charybdis, between whom Ulysses had to safely navigate. Finding the middle path and steering your way on the middle path is essential for happiness and success.

The term 'Middle Path' is inspired from ancient ideas of balance. Buddhist literature exemplifies the idea and I quote from what the Buddha has said:

You must never forget my following words.
In times of success,
People climb up the stairs of success.

But you must remember that those stairs
Are simultaneously heading down towards failure.
Therefore, do not forget,
That the roads to success and failure
Are opposite sides of the same coin.
This truth becomes more evident
As the slope becomes steeper.
People who do not succeed, seldom find failure.
However, those who experience many successes,
Shall experience many failures.
You must understand this truth of the Middle Way.

I thank the many colleagues with whom I have had the privilege of working. Without intending it, they taught me those lessons which no school can teach.

I am deeply grateful to three stalwarts in the field of management who have taken the time to embellish the book with their perspectives as foreword. Thanks Paul, Ram and Shantanu.

I thank my publisher, Krishan Chopra, at HarperCollins India for egging me on and giving me his ideas on how to shape the book.

I am indebted to Sudha Raghavendran, who has diligently worked on this book, my third one, always insisting that she remain unnamed. But this time, I have decided to ignore her request!

My loyal assistant, Theresa Sequeira, deserves my formal vote of thanks for her ungrudging nature and beatific smile every one of those million times I changed something or the other in the book.

Lastly I express gratitude to my dear family. After one book was launched, with great relief, they would assume that it would be the last. Then they would watch me go for the next one. They do not know it, but they are the ones who have inspired me. Thank you, family.

I remember what Sir Winston Churchill wrote about writing a book: 'Writing a book is an adventure. To begin with, it is a toy, an amusement; then it becomes a mistress, then a master, and then finally, a tyrant.'

Mumbai   R. GOPALAKRISHNAN
30 July 2012

1

UNDERSTAND THE PATH

Arup's Story

*The true test of a first-class mind is the ability to hold two
diametrically opposite thoughts in the mind and
yet be able to function.*

—Aristotle

Almost everybody you know is a boss to some people but a
subordinate to some others. There are innumerable books
on how to be an effective boss. There are few books on how to
be an effective subordinate. Why are there so many books,
magazine articles and advisors on how to be a successful leader,
on how to achieve phenomenal results, on how to inspire
subordinates, on how you can put the social network of the
company to your advantage, and on how to work your way up
to the C-suite and so few on being a good subordinate is a
question to ponder.

1

However, you also need books and advice on how to be a good subordinate, on how to be viewed favourably by your bosses, on how you can navigate the politics of your employer's company. Who is going to tell you about these things? You have not seen a serious book on how to be a good subordinate, have you? And only if you have been a good subordinate can your career progress.

To end up as a boss, you first need to be a great subordinate.

You are young when you set out to build a career. You clearly remember your early days of company work as a professional manager—huge hope, burning ambition, energizing anticipation and deep anxiety, all rolled into one. It is a time when you are, and when you genuinely feel that you are, everybody's subordinate.

Then begin the lessons of experience—new roles, new bosses and unexpected challenges.

Doing things, learning lessons, doing more things and learning again, and so the cycle goes on, endlessly. Many years later, these experiences can be recounted as anecdotes, many with emotional resonance and deep feeling.

As the years progress, you begin to understand that there is the formal organization and the informal organization: its structure, its practices and its people, who reports to whom, who matters, who is pulling his or her weight and who is not, who your boss is and his or her relationship to others in the organization, who owes what to whom and so on.

Early on, you begin to understand what output you are required to deliver: simple things like work timing, dos and don'ts at work, how work gets done, what targets you are required to achieve and by when, and how you should measure your performance. In due course, you start developing ideas about what you can expect from the organization and your bosses, what are your entitlements, what training courses you can attend and what sort of career paths you might aspire for.

ASYMMETRY MARKS YOUR CAREER GRAPH

As part of my training sessions, I conduct an exercise on the subject of expectations. What does the boss owe you? What do you owe the boss? After compiling answers over several hundred candidates' responses, I find that people list nine expectations from their boss but only four from themselves to their boss!

The nine things that managers feel that their boss owes them are: feedback, empowerment, coaching, transparency, recognition, opportunity, clear tasks, access and respect for personal time.

The four things that people feel they owe their boss are: one hundred per cent effort, loyalty, honesty and get-it-done results.

When your consciousness and focus in any relationship is driven by what the other person owes you rather than what you owe that person, that is asymmetry; this means that more often than not, you are giving less than what you take out of the relationship. Such unbalanced expectations merit some thought, because the asymmetry is the cause of strife and disappointment.

It is important for any good subordinate to think about the boss's needs as much as he or she would like the boss to think of his or her needs.

UNDERSTANDING THE CAUSES OF ASYMMETRY

To deal with this asymmetry in expectations, you need to appreciate how the expectations develop in the first place. How do expectations from your boss and company build up in your mind? How and when do you develop ideas about what you owe the company and your boss?

Before you joined the company, you might have been told implicitly or through presentations what the system is and how it works. Such discussions are always accompanied by suitable doses of mystery on the ground that 'those are confidential details'. You are advised that your career will automatically develop and that you just need to keep your head down and accomplish your targets. Over time, you start to think of your career as a neatly defined pathway with a map. You never seem to have a clear enough appreciation of what your career path is, or will be. But you are frequently assured that the bosses indeed have one chalked out for you.

You may have a healthy sense of disbelief about how the system works. Yet you soon feel persuaded or even convinced that your bosses and the company owe you not just a living but a career. You traverse your career path with a high degree of awareness and consciousness about your privileges and what others owe you than about your obligations to others. After all your company's HR department has probably explained to you that you are being hired because you are so good. They reiterate that you join their kind of company for a larger career, not merely for a job.

The responsibility of the company for your betterment becomes sharply etched in your mind and takes strong root.

All this while, you think less about your obligation to your bosses and company. You look around to observe the career path of your seniors and formulate your own ideas of what your route could or should be. But, deep within yourself, you know that you do not know how to go about it. But your ambitious eyes are set on the senior roles that the company has. Your dream destination starts to crystallize. Your thoughts start to take shape about the path you might adopt to get to that destination.

It could be you are an engineer, accountant, MBA or a lawyer and you soon become familiar enough with your work environment to articulate lofty concepts about developing a career path, having a clear idea about what you want to achieve, and planning your career milestones.

In a meandering and confounding way, you rush along on your journey, driven a great deal by the possibilities and destinations rather than by immediate challenges. The bosses you work with definitely influence the trajectory of your career.

The word CEO is used to connote the many seniors who influence your work and career. It is not just the immediate person you work for. It includes other seniors with whom you interact and who form a view or judgment about you as a manager. Understanding and responding to what the CEO wants from you is very important to your success and career. An average manager's career lasts about thirty-five years. Every few years, a manager works with a new boss. During a career, the manager might work under twenty people who may influence his or her career quite a lot, say ten direct bosses and the ten bosses of those bosses.

The expectation of the manager from his or her boss is that of perfection, the expectation is that the boss will be a perfect leader, perhaps even mythical. But in reality, that is not how bosses are made. They are human and fallible. Irrespective of what you think of the CEO, you have to accept the CEO as he is.

However, you rarely consider what you owe your bosses. Very likely you feel that if you have done your job diligently, then that is what you owe them. But does the boss have other needs? Does the CEO have an agenda of priorities? Does he have any insecurities or points to prove with *his* boss? Should such thoughts bother you at all?

As you grow in experience, you begin to realize the extent of influence that the CEO has on your career. You recall some CEOs with warmth and others with a tinge of animosity, but you remember all the CEOs you worked with. If you can learn to read what your CEO wants from you, it might just give you the opportunity to be better tuned to his needs.

CEOs do four things that affect the manager's career journey: they guide, they judge, they coach and they speak about the employee with influential people. These are the ways by which the CEO has a strong influence on the manager's career.

As you enter mid-career, you realize the paradox that youth was wasted on you at a young age!

It is part of your job to work at understanding your superior and help to get the best out of his and your efforts. Just as there are no perfect bosses, there are no perfect subordinates. But you need to think about how to be a good subordinate rather than just hope you will automatically become one. This book is about how to be an outstanding subordinate to the many bosses you will have during your career.

ARUP'S CAREER STORY

Here is the real-life story of Arup (name changed)—not an unusual or instructional career, but with features that you are bound to recognize as having been part of your own career journey.

Arup was born to a schoolteacher and his wife. He had three brothers and a sister. The family lived in a small town where they had a modest home and considerable respect. Schoolteachers were well respected in the community in those days. There was not much money to go around, but enough to do the most important things. Here are some stories from Arup's childhood.

BOX 1.1: ARUP'S CHILDHOOD

Being part of a schoolteacher's family meant that education was given a great deal of importance. Regular attendance and superlative performance in exams were high priorities. A solid and good education was placed on a pedestal. Facilities in the small school were limited, but they served the purpose.

The eldest was a brother, considerably older than his siblings. He became a schoolteacher. The parents died early, and the young family became dependent on the earnings of the eldest brother. He became a father figure to the siblings and was deeply respected and loved. He stayed single so that the youngsters could advance their education within the available financial resources.

Arup was the third child in the family with only one brother after him in the family hierarchy. Arup's childhood was characterized by minor ailments and unlike his elder siblings, he used to fall sick often. In line with the social beliefs in those days, he was encouraged to participate in demanding physical activities, which would strengthen his body and improve his resistance to disease. Arup did this quite well because he resented being teased and called a weakling.

When he was in his early teens, on one occasion, he was playing football. His friends poked fun at his stamina. He was so incensed by the teasing that he picked up a fight, not casual word-slinging, but a physical one. He demonstrated a surprising physical brutishness, to the amazement of the school and community, as he sought to redeem his position as a sportsman. He would rise early in the morning and go for long runs and physical training in the local gymnasium, morning after morning. This built up his stamina and also his capacity for strong and laborious physical activity. He would exercise morning after morning in the hope that he would learn to achieve more out of the same effort, thereby showing great discipline and consistency.

As his eldest brother recalled later, Arup developed a glare in his eyes, which almost seemed to say, 'Do you want to take me on?' It seemed to be a look meant to promote self-defence rather than convey aggression for the sake of being aggressive.

After Arup completed school successfully in the small town, his satisfied family sent him for a degree to the nearest big town. In the college hostel, he acquired the reputation of being a persistent student. He always wanted to reflect on how he could apply his knowledge and pushed himself to learn by doing so. If there were two ways to solve a problem, one being direct but tough and the second being indirect but soft, he would invariably choose the former. He became Mr Direct Problem Solver!

He was quick to grasp new concepts and could express his thoughts with great clarity. He was deeply conscious of his small-town background and late introduction to the English language. He would spend hours writing his notes and letters in English. On each occasion, he made a genuine effort to write more succinctly and differently from an earlier occasion. He was always in possession of a pencil and an eraser so that he could make modifications to his composition without rewriting everything. This was long before word processors and laptops!

THE BEGINNING OF A CAREER

These qualities made him a potentially good recruit for a management career, one that could also be financially rewarding. So he went to a productivity-consulting company where he could secure a trainee's job.

His bosses liked his disciplined approach to consulting work and the positive impression he created. But Arup wanted to do things himself rather than be a mere consultant. He had a great need to show that he could do things in a better manner.

A little more money was also welcome to support his brother to meet the mounting family expenses. So he went to see an avuncular relative, who encouraged Arup to apply for a job in a manufacturing company. Arup did so and was selected.

Throughout his life, Arup showed great respect and gratitude to this 'uncle' for giving him a break and introducing him to the new company.

For the next ten years, Arup worked in the factories of this company. His first boss was the head of the Factory Productivity Department and was a foreign national. His educational and intellectual endowments were rather average in Arup's opinion. However, the boss had solid and practical experience. Arup worked diligently and learnt what he could. But he kept his less-than-flattering opinion about his boss to himself and displayed great courtesy and regard: it was not difficult to do so in a newly independent India where foreigners were somehow still regarded as being superior. Above all, it made sense for his career!

Arup was eager to move into more action-orientation, which meant moving to the manufacturing shop. He got a break when he was asked to work as the shop floor manager of a rather sweaty and messy department. In this role, he had to persuade men who were more than twice his age how to work as a team and deliver even better results than they had been doing so far.

He did not find his work creative but the act of motivating his team to accomplish tough goals excited him. He learnt the art of communicating crisply and of writing precise notes about what additional resources his department would require or what needed fixing.

Within five years, Arup did a lot of new things in a part of the factory which was considered to be dull. His middle-aged boss spoke well of Arup's rather direct and refreshing approach to problem solving. His boss's colleagues began to notice Arup and his work. Some of them had their eye on the young man for a future vacancy in their own department.

Arup got a break as a senior leader when he was selected to lead a small team of shop managers in the same factory. Arup could sense that he had done well thus far. He could identify many areas of inefficiency in the factory and was aching to get his hands around every part of the unit. He could not understand why his peers were not dealing expeditiously with the issues and inefficiencies that he could see very clearly. He concluded that they were not sufficiently enterprising in their attitude and lacked the risk-taking ability and the inner drive to change things. These were two qualities he had personally set a lot of store by.

He secretly wondered how these bosses had got to where they had reached. Would the company not be very different if young and energetic managers like himself were given an opportunity to be in senior management?

Thanks to an encouraging and supportive boss, he made dramatic changes and improvements in the production processes of his own department. Although he was exposed to the same facts as others, Arup demonstrated a unique way of viewing issues and crafting solutions. He just seemed to learn more than the others, time after time.

He also showed signs of impatience with peers and subordinates with lesser comprehension, energy or drive. His matter-of-fact and blunt ways of describing an issue and articulating possible solutions was a little annoying to his peers. In their opinion, he spoke like a person who knew everything. On occasion, he was perceived as being condescending or rude. But on the whole, he was considered a leader who delivered results because his peers realized that this guy was indeed different. He seemed to have a distinctive manner about him.

ARUP GETS A BREAK

A company director felt that Arup should run his own medium-sized factory independently. This was the break Arup did not plan for or expect. Obviously he had caught the eye of his big boss. The seniors did recognize and discuss among themselves Arup's tendency to be abrasive but were willing to make allowance for it. After all, a line manager must have some bite as well as bark to run a factory, they thought. Anyway, Arup delivered solid performance and additionally, he was young, just in his early thirties.

With his own factory to run, Arup became a sort of king in his own empire. His immediate boss was several hundred miles away. To the 300 people in that factory, Arup was the emperor. His writ ruled on whatever happened or had to happen. He seemed to have unquestioned authority within his kingdom. And Arup loved it that way. He became very self-confident as he talked to his employees, helped them solve their maintenance or manpower problems and stretched the factory assets to new levels of cost efficiency and machine productivity.

Further, he had to interact with the local government officials. To them, Arup was Mr Company, whether it was the District Magistrate, the Police Superintendent, the Excise Tax Officer and so on. He learnt the art of business advocacy. He did not have a positive view of the intellectual calibre of some of these public officials or their level of probity. He would patiently explain to them what they could do as part of their legitimate duties that would help his factory to do better and contribute more to the local economy.

For the first time in his career, Arup learnt that his success depended on his ability to influence people whom he did not control and on whom he had no formal or implied authority.

In this role, Arup had for the first time to deal with a remote head office. He had to assess the local situation and act, but he also needed to consult and carry with his decision various functional heads in the head office. These HO folks, in his opinion, had a cushy role. They did not seem to have any responsibility to decide or to deliver, but they seemed to have infinite authority to block him from doing anything. All that they had to do, in his view, was to ask a few clever questions or raise a few relevant points. What a role they had! HO was a bloody nuisance and would the company not be better off if its size were slashed to half its current size!

Arup's Search for More Meaning from Work

Arup's career was progressing very smoothly. Here he was, just under forty, heading a medium-sized factory in a large manufacturing company. However, three things started to bother the impatient Arup.

Arup was bothered by his perception that the company had lethargic decision making and poor action orientation. There were many HO managers who could prevent him from achieving his goals, yet bore no responsibility for meeting targets. He was also apprehensive whether his company would allow a middle-class, small-town engineer to grow in an environment where foreign education and polished manners seemed to matter a lot. These issues started to bother him.

At this time, he was vulnerable to career predators. He was not unhappy enough to actively seek a new job but he was not happy enough to avoid the sidelong glances of people who had jobs to offer. And one such opportunity came his way.

His wife's uncle, who had set up a very successful business in manufacturing, wanted to professionalize his firm. His firm had a foreign collaboration; it had recently gone public through a listing and was very successful in the marketplace. The firm had built up a terrific reputation for putting quality products into the market, with considerable marketing savvy to boot.

In short, the firm was a family business with an urgent need to professionalize its management. Arup's fit into this need was a perfect match. He was being offered a director's role. Arup felt that this could give him the degree of freedom that he so desperately needed—to fly, to soar and do the big things that he had always dreamed about.

He would not have to suffer the head office fools as he himself would now be in the HO. It would be a different HO! The listed company could boast of having brought in a management professional from a top-class and reputed firm. So everybody could win. The money was also attractive enough for Arup to consider the positive effect on his not-so-rich family. He made the change.

Arup's employer was very sorry to lose him. The seniors tried hard to hold him back but Arup had decided that he would leave—albeit in a perfectly amicable way. Arup made sure that none of his bosses got any wrong impression. He was not resigning in a huff, nor was he contemptuous of the company. He gave the impression that he was merely helping an uncle while advancing his career. In short, he left the company with a lot of goodwill.

In a family-managed company, who would be his bosses and colleagues, especially when he was a member of the family? Several cousins for sure, but otherwise mostly others. But it was odd to Arup that there were 'family members' and 'others'.

Did it really matter? He wondered what it would be like to work in a family-managed company (see Box 1.2).

BOX 1.2: THE FAMILY-MANAGED COMPANY EXPERIENCE

The family members and the others were like two different classes of people. The dynamics of how they interacted among themselves and with each other, the unstated rules of engagement and the distance between the two classes were intriguing to Arup. His boss now was an uncle. His peer now was a cousin. Arup had some difficulty interpreting every office interaction.

Some made sense to interpret as between colleagues and some as between cousins. Over time, everything got tangled, at least in Arup's mind. Sometimes people not directly connected with the office would get involved. For example, Arup was furious one day when his wife broached a particular office situation to him, her source being her sister-in-law. This was no way to work, Arup fumed.

Gradually, Arup found his effectiveness thwarted by what he called 'family politics'. It took Arup only two years to get tired of the situation. By personality, he was an impatient sort of bloke.

His upbringing had produced influences that made him outwardly aggressive and sharp-tongued. He was an incessant workaholic who sought perfection. With experience, he had become intolerant of sloppiness in others. This was certainly not a combination of qualities that would help him survive in a family-managed business. His chagrin was enhanced when his wife told him that in every office, there would be politics, so how did it matter whether it was 'office politics' or 'family politics'? To cap it all, his wife had begun to advise him that he should become more adaptive by demonstrating some flexibility and avoid treating everybody around as a dimwit! Really, this was getting to be too much!

Now he began to display a trait more visibly—rage. He could not hold back his anger or his feelings. He often spoke sharply, almost rebuking people. Relations at office drifted from bad to worse.

Within two years, Arup decided that he could not carry on. He suddenly preferred the somewhat slow-moving, non-interfering bosses from his earlier company. Luckily, his relationship with his bosses there had not soured.

When he approached them to explore the possibility of return, they engaged with him—in fact, they engaged so enthusiastically, that the conversations could have gone straight to his head. They actually welcomed Arup back into a more senior role than the one he had left a couple of years earlier. Arup was relieved that his misery could be brought to a speedy conclusion.

POISED FOR A LEAP IN CAREER

Back in his old company, Arup was on familiar terrain and could resume old relationships. He could hit the ground running. And that is what he did. He turned the workplace upside down, making deep changes and impactful decisions. His bosses had bet on him and backed him, not only to prove their bet right, but also because he was attacking outstanding issues directly, the kind of issues that few others would dare to deal with aggressively. Arup was on a roll.

Within the next four years, he had worked through two other roles. During these four years, he took great care to maintain excellent relations upwards. His seniors saw a thrusting, achieving leader for the future. But several of his peers and subordinates hated his style. He was perceived to be impatient, rude and brutish in his ways, almost to the point of being considered self-centred. Nearly everyone hated his brusque methods but each person adjusted in his or her own way. Some quit, some suffered him and others tried to keep out of his way.

And after four years, guess what happened? He was appointed CEO. His seniors looked forward to an era of change and challenge. His subordinates and critics were apprehensive about his ways. But not one of them had any doubt that he would change and shape things in his own distinctive way.

And that is exactly what Arup did. Over the next ten years, he led the company to march to a completely different drumbeat. In his assessment, the company needed to do three things very differently. And he led from the front to accomplish dramatic results in each of these.

First, he found much of the company's business infested with government interference. He had learned earlier in his career that a good business manager must learn to work in three circles. In the initial years, he learns to master work in the inner circle where the targets and resources are within his control. In the middle part of his career, he works in the centre circle in which he still has to accomplish results even though the resources are not entirely within his command. In the senior roles, he has to work in the outer circle where he has to accomplish results with little or no control whatsoever on the resources or people. Arup found his agenda rich in the outer circle. He used all the skills of charm and diplomacy to wrench the company out of the government's interference.

Second, the trade unions everywhere were on a high. Factory after factory was being bullied and held to ransom by militant labour. Arup confronted his company union's militancy with his own brand of aggression. Within five years, his company had the recognized union busy in the law courts, while he got ahead with reshaping and reorganizing the company operations. The leadership of the trade unions now realized that the new CEO would fight them tooth for tooth without respite and unrelentingly.

Third and last, he altered his executive team's mindset from behaving as though they were helpless about their circumstances. He would deploy what he called the 5Cs— communicate, convince, cajole, coerce and finally crucify the executives—if they did not respond at some stage.

'Get hold of your future, or else someone else will get hold of it,' he would thunder long before Jack Welch said similar things at GE. His shareholders loved him because the company earnings shot up. His peers and subordinates were fearful of his ways but they could not help admiring Arup's focus on getting results.

At a personal level, Arup was a very different person from the tyrant he was at work. When his elder brother passed away, he was crushed. He demonstrated his devotion to him in every possible way. He was deeply aware of the breaks and privileges that had come his way. He tried to share his earnings for the benefit of less privileged relations and institutions. He showed his generosity to others in so many ways that many who knew both sides of him found it difficult to reconcile the two Arups.

When Arup retired, he was given a fabulous farewell— eulogies, bountiful memorabilia of his association with the company and the heaviest of picture albums and flower garlands. But within a few months, employees threw up their straw hats to celebrate the departure of a leader who, according to them, had destroyed the peace of mind of too many.

The company had not seen the likes of Arup earlier. Arup was a small-town lad who made it quite big in management. He was bright, hard-working, ambitious, persistent . . . and could command many more adjectives of virtue. He was also hard as nails, brash, outspoken, matter of fact . . . and could command other adjectives of virtue or vice, depending on the circumstances. He was a solid doer, determined to get things done, accomplish relentlessly, challenge and be challenged.

The CEOs he worked with loved his results. He aimed high and delivered time and again. His colleagues admired his intellect and his thrusting style. They admired how hard he worked, day after day. In fact they were secretly jealous of his energetic approach to work. How could he accomplish so much more than they could?

His subordinates were scared of him. He could at times border on being rude and insulting. Some felt that it was an issue of style and that he was intrinsically a good person. If one understood this, he could be a boss one could learn a lot from.

Others felt that he was just a plain and simple bully. They did not feel it worthwhile or necessary to give him any benefit of doubt. For these people, he was not the kind of boss they wanted to work with.

But Arup was not the kind to leave a company as he found it.

This narration is not intended to illustrate a right or wrong way of developing or managing a career. This is a bland narration of a successful manager's life, his bosses and his career. If there were a framework to understand how Arup understood what his CEO wanted and adapted to that need, we may be able to derive a lesson or two about how to navigate a career. The basis of a framework is explored in the next chapter.

2

ADAPT THROUGH THE JOURNEY

If you have a correct statement, then the opposite of a correct statement is of course an incorrect statement, a wrong statement. But when you have a deep truth, then the opposite of a deep truth may again be a deep truth

—Niels Bohr

The great physicist Niels Bohr spoke about two kinds of truth, deep truth and shallow truth. The function of science is to eliminate the deep truth. If the truth is shallow, it allows us to wade in periodically and seek fresh viewpoints and hypotheses, which are most important in establishing new frontiers of knowledge.

A career is a journey of constant and continuous learning (see Box 2.1). When you begin your career, metaphorically you stand on the shore of the ocean. You sail out into the shallow waters when you are assigned known problems with known

21

solutions. These are problems which you solve with the resources specifically assigned to you; for example, to produce a target quantity and quality of product in every shift within specified efficiencies of manpower and materials. Recall how Arup got his first and early career break when he was asked to run the shop floor of a rather messy department.

BOX 2.1: YOU SAIL INTO THE OCEAN FROM KNOWN KNOWNS TO UNKNOWN UNKNOWNS

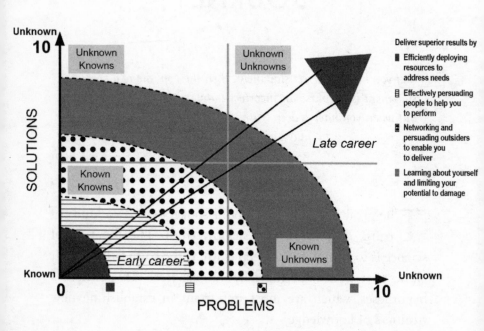

As you move deeper into the ocean, the nature of the problems encountered alters. Sometimes there are known problems with unknown solutions; at other times, the problem is unknown, but the solutions are known. Such problems typically have a lot of uncertainty due to markets or the behaviour of people.

For example, you have to confront a difficult sales supervisor with regard to work quality or a disciplinary matter. He may be a person who has more experience than you have and who is much older than you. Or, for example, you have to launch a new product concept into a market about which there is not much experience within the company.

Arup's story reveals how he had to adapt and change, as he moved to run a factory which was far away from the HO, and where he had to behave as Mr Company. He had to learn to operate effectively even though he was not impressed with the quality of some of his head office colleagues. (Most of the readers would agree with this view, until they begin to work at head office!)

Finally, the manager sails into uncharted waters which are deep and risky. He encounters unknown problems with unknown solutions. He has to think, consult, experiment, learn and advance, while, all through, he has to give his subordinates the impression that he knows exactly what he is doing! He also has to influence people on whom he has no jurisdiction or control. Yet he has to solve real problems and deliver real results.

Reflect on what Arup had to do when he was appointed CEO of the company. He had decided that the company had to be transformed and had to learn to march to a completely different drumbeat. However, this involved persuading and cajoling government departments and taking on the labour unions. These were very different tasks from the ones he had addressed earlier in his career. What he had done for success in the past would not work for him at the more senior levels.

'PRACTICAL INTELLIGENCE' MEANS STEERING BETWEEN SCYLLA AND CHARYBDIS

During my long career, I have made several errors of judgment, I can say that finding an optimum path between opposing demands requires practical intelligence. Webster's dictionary defines intelligence as the 'capacity for learning, reasoning, understanding, and similar forms of mental activity; aptitude in grasping truths, relationships, facts, meanings etc.' The dictionary definition captures how we commonly think of intelligence. But people understand intelligence in different ways (see Box 2.2).

BOX 2.2

Intelligence Quotient[1]

In 1904, the French Minister for education approached psychologist Alfred Binet to devise some system to classify children according to their capacity to learn. This was required as a general intelligence measure. Modern IQ tests have all been born out of adaptations of the original Alfred Binet research work. The testing was based on judgment, comprehension, and

---

reasoning, all of these being dependent on verbal skills. These are the foundations of intelligence testing even today.

Over a period of time, it was realized that IQ tests were inaccurate predictors of future behaviour and of success and failure. This was because what makes for success in later life was a very complicated combination of personality and situational factors.

Emotional Intelligence[2]

Around 1995, a psychologist, Daniel Goleman, introduced this expression. He said that EQ was quite independent of IQ. His point was that personal skills such as tact, human interactions, and such emotional and social variables together constitute emotional intelligence. To get a more reliable predictor of future success, Goleman felt that IQ and EQ had to be viewed together. You could be exceptionally gifted in general intelligence, but not well endowed in judging personal relations, as was the case with Einstein.

Social Intelligence[3]

This was a follow-on concept, again from Goleman. The most fundamental discovery, according to the author, was that humans are designed for sociability. They are constantly engaging in a sort of mental or neural ballet that connects your brain to the brains of those around you.

Political Intelligence[4]

Roderick Kramer is a social psychologist and a professor at Stanford Business School. He used the expression political intelligence. He found that though there had been a strong advocacy in favour of humane leaders with excellent soft skills, the reality was that successful leaders tended to be bullies who intimidated their teams to deliver. Leaders with political intelligence are very good at sizing up people for their weaknesses rather than their strengths. And having sized them up for weaknesses, they intimidate and bully subordinates by playing on those weaknesses. You can think of Jack Welch, Al Dunlap, Ed Zander and many other examples from the writings on American management.

Among Indian political leaders, you might count Mrs Indira Gandhi and her son, Sanjay Gandhi. Among business leaders, you might include A.N. Haksar, T. Thomas and V. Krishnamurthy. They were hugely successful leaders professionally who demonstrated great political intelligence.

Multiple Intelligence

Prof. Howard Gardner is a very insightful researcher and writer on human intelligence and learning. He is a professor at the Harvard Graduate School of Education.

He coined a new term to evaluate intelligence and achievement and he called this multiple intelligence. To my mind, MI is the ability to use IQ and EQ together within a specific situation or context. Many situations require the use of one's IQ and EQ in some balance between two opposing courses of action, for example, being firm and flexible at the same time or being focussed and open-minded at the same time.

Gardner later updated his view and stated that a person will require developing and relying on five minds to be well prepared for the future. He called these the disciplined mind, the synthesizing mind, the creating mind, the respectful mind and the ethical mind. A practical understanding of Gardner's concepts helps me to provide a framework to understand how Arup might have developed the ability to figure out and deliver what his CEO wanted of him.

Practical Intelligence

In the course of life, irrespective of which profession you might be in, there is great need for practical intelligence. This is not a researched term as some of the more technical terms described above are. It is what you and I know is necessary to succeed. I am unable to define what exactly it is but I recognize it when I encounter it in someone. It is perhaps a combination of all of the above.

As you traverse your career path, you have to learn to adapt the skills that you have acquired and the manner in which you deploy those skills. Such adaptation calls for practical intelligence. You tend to watch successful leaders and selectively emulate some or all of their leadership practices in your quest for success. However, each success story is set within a context. If the context changes, the perception of success also changes.

For example, Arup was known to be abrasive with his peers and subordinates. Yet he seemed to be successful in the context of his work and times. It may well be that the same practices used by Arup would be resisted strongly in today's times.

Hence, as physicist Niels Bohr observed about truths in general, there is no deep truth with respect to leadership. There are only shallow truths and the function of leadership anecdotes and theories is to eliminate the so-called deep truths.

You also have to deliver what the CEO wants. But how do you figure out what precisely the CEO wants?

You learn it through implicit means. Some expectations can be written explicitly, for instance, Annual Targets and Key Result Areas, but there will still be limitations. Those with experience know that targets can never be devoid of ambiguity.

The truth is that soft factors do matter: did you use the right approach while getting the work done, what was the extent and impact on colleagues, how did you inspire subordinates? These are never specified explicitly or in advance. The CEO's expectations in these matters are tactile and invisible. The manager has to sense them and figure them out.

Apart from the CEO's expectations being unspecific, they are also positioned at some undefined middle point which seems to embrace two opposite positions. Bosses expect you to get work done, but without upsetting others. Bosses expect you to set challenging and stretching goals, but targets are sacrosanct and must be met. Bosses expect you to work as hard as it takes to deliver work on time, but they also want you to get home at a reasonable hour and take good care of your family.

Finding the middle path is like the challenge faced by Ulysses. On his return home, Ulysses was caught between Scylla (a monster posing a threat) and Charybdis (a whirlpool being another kind of life threat) as he was navigating a narrow passage in the Aegean Sea. Your career is very often about finding and traversing carefully the narrow path between two approaches. Box 2.3 shows the difficult path leaders have to traverse.

BOX 2.3

Coriolanus

There is a story from ancient Rome about Coriolanus, Shakespeare's tragic general. He was a great warrior, he had a very strong moral compass, and he was considered honest to the core. Notwithstanding his many talents, he had a tremendous flaw. He just did not connect with the Roman people. Mistakenly, he thought that if he mingled with them, it would be a form of pandering to them and above all, a sacrifice of his integrity. His mother begged him to do so but to no avail. Coriolanus failed to notice that Rome was changing into a state where the common folk mattered.

Shakespeare opens his tragedy with the Romans on the street being addressed by a mutinous citizen. He says that Coriolanus is the chief enemy of the people. If they could kill him, they would have corn at a reasonable price. Finally in their fury, the people of Rome did kill Coriolanus.

Jamil Mahuad

Another story, which is more modern, is about Jamil Mahuad. He had been the successful mayor of Quito province in Ecuador, and was extremely popular because he walked around the city to meet voters and solved their problems.

He was so successful that he became the president of the country. Aides and assistants brought issues and recommended solutions as the immediate and efficient remedy. Inadvertently, Jamil Mahuad stopped doing what gave him his initial success, that is, being visible to his people, providing hope in the face of the numerous problems and communicating about why his government needed to modernize the economy.

Initially, things went well. Unluckily, the country was then visited by an El Nino storm, followed by inflation, huge foreign debt, bankrupt banks and a whole host of problems. It is not that these were sudden developments; rather they were issues waiting to be solved.

There was great pressure on this 'proven leader' to deliver. He cut government salaries, cancelled orders for the purchase of defence equipment, reduced recruitment into the army and so on. These were probably correct solutions in the 'technical' sense, but their implementation lacked the buy-in of people.

On 21 January 2000, a coalition of military officers and demonstrators forced Mahuad out of office after just one year. He had lost contact with his people. He realized that only later.

An Example of Practical Intelligence in Work-Life Balance

I recall a video clip from GE that was used at the Harvard Advanced Management Program. In that video clip, Jack Welch is seen in a conversation with some upcoming managers at the Crotonville Training Centre. One of the managers asks the chairman a question, 'How do you balance the commitment to the company with the demands of the family? I find it very difficult to do justice to both and I just cannot seem to get the work-life balance right.'

Welch looks deep into the young manager's face and asks what the problem is. Welch states that even as chairman, he works the needed fourteen hours in the day but that he also plays golf over the weekend and enjoys his time with his family. If he could do so as chairman, the young man should have fewer problems in achieving work-life balance. Next question!

You should have seen the manager's expression captured by the video camera—he looked dazed and slighted, both rolled into one.

The issue of work-life balance is real and increasingly important. Jack Welch may be perceived to have dismissed his young subordinate's question, but the problem on the ground for the young manager is a real one. The competitiveness of the marketplace does demand more and more 24x7 emotionally connected managers. Simultaneously, the pressure at home also requires the manager to be a hugely involved spouse. For one, both spouses are working and following a career path. Less and less help and time are available to supplement the increasing needs of the family and lifestyle. A great sense of social egalitarianism between the spouses is taken for granted nowadays. So managing the work-life balance is quite complicated.

Erik Sorensen, the CEO of Vault, a Web resource for career management and job search information, has addressed this issue with a sense of practical intelligence.[5] Welch had told the Society for Human Resource Management in 2009 that 'there is no such thing as work-life balance ... there are work-life choices, and you make them, and they have consequences'. This upset HR professionals as too female executives, for reasons that are not hard to find.

Welch was making an obvious point, he says. Any manager has only a finite number of hours. He or she has to figure out the most suitable way to use them. The 'limited hours' concept pertains not only to the physical clock time but also to the emotional time of the manager.

If your company permits flexi-hours, unpaid sabbatical or maternity leave time, then you are lucky and you should use the facilities fully. But having made that choice, it is inevitable that it will have some consequences, according to Sorensen. If you are not there to help your boss or to lead your people, howsoever well placed the reasons may be, then it is going to be hard to earn that promotion compared to another manager who has made a different choice. The hullabaloo about Jack Welch's statement may have more to do with his perceived dismissal of the concept of work-life balance.

This is an example of applying practical intelligence to the issue.

For the practical person, a cursory understanding of the theory is adequate. Practical and real-life examples that follow in the subsequent chapters may help you mull over this idea of practical intelligence. The stories and their lessons are bound to evoke in the reader the sense that he or she has been through such a journey.

Readers who are interested in the theoretical basis for the five minds (disciplined, synthesizing, creative, respectful and ethical) should read Harvard academic Howard Gardner.[6] A summary of Gardner's concepts appears in Box 2.4.

BOX 2.4: FIVE MINDS FOR THE FUTURE

Disciplined Mind

Gardner's basic concept is etched in my mind through the sequence of grasp-perform-learn. He termed this in more technical terms as 'performance of understanding'. If a person can grasp a particular situation, perform an appropriate task and gain a skill out of doing so, then he or she would have demonstrated a disciplined mind. Reflect on Arup's story.

The same facts about the manufacturing process were imparted to all the young managers, including Arup. The same blokes taught Arup the same things. Arup seemed to learn a lot more about the manufacturing process than many of his contemporaries. One attribute of the disciplined mind is this capability to delve deeper and deeper into a 'specialization' and keep learning.

But Arup also seemed to learn different things. How come? It was the outcome of his disciplined mind.

After learning the facts, Arup would apply those facts within a context, try out something differently and learn new things. For example, if one particular product required a maturing cycle of eight weeks, thus tying up company money and working capital, Arup would ask, could the maturing process be changed? Or if the given wisdom was that the union had to be tackled in a particular way, he would think through whether there was an alternative.

In short, such a way of thinking led Arup to a distinctive point of view. Arup learnt more than his peers, not because he had access to any different facts, but because he became a reflective practitioner of his newly acquired knowledge. This kind of instinct comes from a disciplined mind.

Synthesizing Mind

As the label suggests, this is the ability to bring disparate items of knowledge and information into a new combination, which leads to an insight. As Howard Gardner has written, at the basic level, it requires the ability to set a goal, build on a particular idea, select a way to deal with it, and articulate the details of the plan. Arup was excellent at these activities as his story demonstrates time and again. When he moved into the family-managed business environment, he could quickly identify the applicability of managerial systems and processes from his earlier experience. That he could not fully succeed in doing so is less important than to know that he tried to apply them.

Like anybody else, Arup would view each challenge through the unique lens of his own experiences. Based on that assessment, several jigsaw pieces of judgment would form in his mind, which he synthesized into a pattern.

It is important to note that while the disciplined mind requires the practitioner to delve deeper and deeper into the specialization, the synthesizing mind requires the practitioner to swim across specializations. Synthesizing means being a generalist. It would appear that we need a specialization in becoming a generalist, as mentioned by educationist Vartan Gregorian in his article in *Chronicle of Higher Education*, 4 June 2004.

Creating Mind

The creating mind sees and perceives things that others are not able to see or perceive. Typically a practitioner in one domain (for example, Einstein in physics) argues a different perspective on a problem (nature of energy) and, over a period of time, others in the domain start to see things very differently in the light of that perspective. The creating person often stands out of the pack and thinks, behaves and acts differently.

In the field of management, think of the creating influences of Peter Drucker, Michael Porter and C.K. Prahalad. The creating mind is usually very active at a younger age when the mind is innocent and open. As Sigmund Freud put it, 'When I was young, ideas came to me; as I age, I must go halfway to meet them.'

Using these ideas with respect to Arup, you can

recognize the vigour of his creating mind. His story suggests that he was restless, that he would think up new ways to solve existing problems and that he would be impatient to try solutions. Out of all that activity, he seemed to learn lessons and skills. Even in the matter of dealing with the labour union, he adopted the same approach as he did in solving a factory productivity problem.

Respectful Mind

The word respect is used by Gardner to connote tolerance. There are, and will be, differences among people, but he has termed the ability to tolerate and live with differences as respect. It is a humanistic value, so its importance and value seem unnecessary to debate. It is a virtue. Researchers who study team work conclude that the success of teams depends more on mutual respect and management skills than excellence in technical skills.

The world of business, however, is replete with stories of successful bosses who treated their subordinates ruthlessly and rudely. Ambitious and young managers may even adopt such practices as though they represent a mantra for success. Consider the stories told in business books about 'neutron' Jack Welch and 'chainsaw' Al Dunlap or the viewpoint expressed in business magazines that in times of rapid change, it is essential to be ruthless.

No human being is 'perfect' so far as being respectful is concerned at all times and under all circumstances.

Disrespect can be shown verbally and non-verbally. In fact, the non-verbal forms of disrespect can be considered to be more disrespectful.

There are some who are open about their feelings and express those feelings verbally—personally speaking, these types do leave me a bit troubled because they are disrespectful, but I cope because I know that what they mean is what they say. Then there are those who hide their feelings and leave you guessing, and they communicate those feelings non-verbally—these types bother me because I am never sure what they mean and how I should relate to them!

Arup's story suggests that he was extremely respectful to his seniors. It was his peers and subordinates with whom he was disrespectful. These are the 'kiss up, kick down' types. Arup was almost reverential when he wanted to get something out of the relationship. Otherwise it appears that he could be quite disrespectful.

Ethical Mind

Here the word ethical is used not in a moralistic sense of right and wrong, but more in a practical sense of what it means to be in this profession (manager, engineer, accountant etc.), what does a person in this profession owe others in society and so on. Every person is the beneficiary of some privileges for having got to where he or she has got to. For example, it may be a privileged education, a lucky break or the munificent guidance of a teacher or mentor.

In the case of Arup, it was his brother to whom he owed so much and also to his uncle who suggested that he apply for a job in some company, which turned out to be a valuable move. An ethical mind docks these privileges and asks the individual a question: in return what do you owe others?

Arup seemed deeply aware of the ethical question as illustrated by his career: his lifelong gratitude to his brother, and his commitment to share his earnings with those less privileged. Both these are the manifestations of the ethical mind.

On the other hand, you read of people who go berserk in their chase of wealth, breaking rules, lying through their teeth and picking unfair quarrels in the process. Those are the antithesis of the ethical mind.

You live your life based on certain assumptions. You test these assumptions with each experience and with each passing day. One such assumption is that the company and your bosses owe you a good career. Another assumption is that all that you owe the bosses is good work and loyalty.

The fact is that there are very few organizations that are geared to understand, let alone deliver, the developmental inputs and processes that you have imagined. You need to revisit the assumptions and prepare to take charge of your development. The skills described by the 4 As— Accomplishment, Affability, Advocacy and Authenticity—are central to your ability to be an outstanding subordinate.

And every great leader was at one time an outstanding subordinate to his or her bosses.

What are these 4 As and how do they show up in your work requirements?

3

THE 4 AS

The Attributes of the High Potential Manager

The best organizations reward bosses for developing leaders—but these organizations are rare. You must take responsibility for your own development.

—Prof. Jay Conger

Much of the management and leadership literature that business people are exposed to tends to be of Anglo-Saxon origin. More specifically, it is American. There is nothing wrong or right about it, but it is important to be conscious of the cultural moorings of the ideas espoused by such writings and books. The ethos in other societies owes its intellectual tradition to a different culture. The display of the 'good attributes' from one culture to another as you climb up the career ladder can have contrary outcomes. One such attribute is the relative weight of being an extrovert or introvert.

In the 1920s, psychologist Carl Jung argued the differences between extroversion and introversion and pleaded for recognition of these as crucial building blocks for the personality. Extroverts are outward-looking, socialize and plunge into things. Introverts are inward-looking, reflective and prefer to observe things rather than plunge into them.

Throughout the twentieth century, initially in America before its spread elsewhere, there was a discount to being an introvert. Leaders and leadership behaviour had to be extrovert. Advertising and salesmanship required a successful person to be in-your-face and it produced an archetype for success. Then there followed the Dale Carnegie wave of confidence and push as desirable personality traits. Recently there have been inspirational speakers like Shiv Khera and Tom Robbins who teach you how to unleash the power within yourself. You should not forget the influence of the B-School archetype: socialize endlessly, be the first to give an opinion (right or wrong), work as a team but exude charisma and border on being loud and gross.

The introvert has become all that is not extrovert. So a reticent leader, a person who thinks before speaking, and who speaks sparsely is seen as 'introverted'. His or her leadership has come to be seen as somehow less effective than that of the extrovert type. This subject has been explored in a fascinating way by Susan Cain, a writer who specializes in psychological non-fiction, in her book.[1]

Therefore career builders should avoid adopting behavioural models of success but rather consider more basic human qualities for success. This chapter is about the 4 As and how they play out in different phases of your career.

I have found it convenient to think of the manager's practical

intelligence through the model of the 4 As, which stand for
Accomplishment, Affability, Advocacy and Authenticity (see
Box 3.1)

BOX 3.1: YOU EVOLVE ALONG A STAIRCASE OF PERSONAL DEVELOPMENT

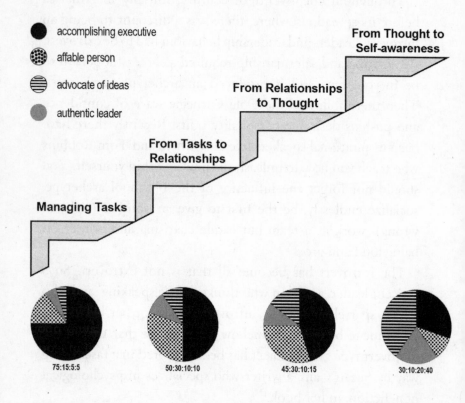

- *Accomplishment* refers to the attribute of delivering results
  reliably. It has to be learned like all skills and practised
  periodically.
- *Affability* is the attribute of developing agreeable

relationships and getting things done in an appropriate manner.

- *Advocacy* is the skill of envisioning new ideas and persuading others to debate those new ideas.
- *Authenticity* is the perception others develop about you, especially subordinates, and about who they think you are.

These four attributes vary in relative importance at each stage of your career journey. There are four stages or discrete steps on your career journey.

Box 3.1 shows that the first step is referred to as *Managing Tasks*, when you have to plan activities to deliver results with the help of people who typically report to you: for example, to achieve sales targets with a team of salesmen, month after month. During this stage, it is crucial to accomplish and to deliver results (75 per cent weightage). The other three As take a lower share of importance. These weights are shown through the moon charts in the diagram.

The second step is when you move *From Tasks to Relationships*. You obviously still need to deliver results, but now you rely on people who do not report to you. You need to get work done, not through hierarchical power, but through lateral relationships. For example, you are the regional manager, but only the sales managers report directly to you; the finance, personnel and legal colleagues report to head office with only a dotted line to you. During this stage, the importance of affability increases compared to the earlier stage.

In both the steps mentioned above, you need what academics recognize as a 'disciplined mind.' (See Box 2.3 in previous chapter on Howard Gardner's five minds.)

The third stage is termed *From Relationship to Thought*. Your

CEO is happy that you are a doer, but he needs to assess the quality of your thinking horsepower. So you are assigned a strategic role such as Marketing Manager, Product Development Manager or Strategy Manager. You rely on a 'synthesizing mind'. Your ability to acquire and synthesize new knowledge becomes very important. At this senior level, you have to imagine the future and create market spaces that are not readily visible to many others, a skill which comes from the 'creating mind'.

On the fourth and final step of the leadership journey, you need to be far more aware of yourself and your society by addressing deep issues about people and community; for example, why does your company exist? What is its unique societal contribution? Does it have ethical or moral standards to live up to, apart from the statutory standards? This kind of thinking emanates from the 'respectful and ethical mind'. At this stage, your authenticity and how people perceive your nature become crucial. Can I trust him? If he asks me to jump, should I jump? These are the sort of questions your subordinates wrestle with.

Before becoming a successful leader, it is essential to be a great subordinate. All successful subordinates are judged by their bosses by observing how well they combine the four qualities of Accomplishment, Affability, Advocacy and Authenticity. These are not static attributes or qualities. They are relative.

You must be 'sufficiently' accomplished in getting things done, you must be affable enough and persuasive enough to be an excellent performer, and you must be 'authentic' enough to be accepted as a peer and as a leader in the roles you perform on the way up.

ACCOMPLISHMENT

Accomplishment means being able to execute with efficiency and to deliver results. It is the most important of the skills that any subordinate has to learn. Simple though it sounds, it is a great weakness among some managers. If execution skills were to be found as abundantly as they are expected, then there would not be so much research and management literature on the subject. There are some reasons why the attribute Accomplishment is not as richly found among managers as one might assume. (See Box 3.2)

BOX 3.2: THE DIFFICULTIES OF ACCOMPLISHMENT

First, managers often hold the view that doing things is the task of lower level people. Salesmen must do the selling, workers and supervisors must do the producing. The manager's task is to do the thinking rather than the doing. This is true but conceals the reality that coordinating is also a part of the thinking task. And coordinating activities which are inherently not well aligned and clear is difficult.

Second, managers have to deliver results without all the resources being directly under their charge. Typically some resources are under their direct control, for example, the people who directly report to the manager; some others are under their influence but not in their control, for example, the finance or human resources functions in a factory or sales office;

and finally, some others are completely outside their control or influence, for example, getting a local licence for one of the activities or public policy matters.

Third, executing complex tasks requires skills in coordination, motivation, review and discipline. Even if one of these is weak, execution suffers. The discipline and granularity required to do all these four jobs is often not strong enough.

Fourth, large organizations provide many hiding places for people who cannot execute well. The art of sexy presentations, the flowery expressions of what are basically excuses and the silver-tongued ability to communicate future promises all combine together to retard execution in companies.

The expectation of being an accomplishing executive stays throughout your working career. There is never a stage when you are not expected to deliver results. As you rise in the organization, you depend more and more on others to deliver. So, like the oxygen required for staying alive, the skill of Accomplishment is a lifelong demand on the manager.

It is not enough to execute, deliver results and demonstrate accomplishment. The results have to be achieved in an acceptable manner. So the method through which you accomplish results becomes the lens through which your actual results are viewed.

Recall the career of Arup (Chapter 1). His seniors noticed that Arup had great ideas and could implement them, but he suffered from a sharp tongue. He could upset people easily.

His subordinates tolerated him out of fear or hated him unequivocally.

Practitioners and thinkers like Larry Bossidy and Ram Charan have pointed out that execution is actually a formal discipline.[2] Execution has three core processes: the people process, the strategy process and the operations process. This discipline is not actually taught in schools of business. And, to be fair, perhaps it is right to argue that such things are difficult to teach. You learn them through constant practice and self-correction with occasional mentoring from coaches—akin to learning sports or music.

Anyone who has worked in organizations recognizes that there is a gap between what the organization knows and what it does. In Unilever, former chairman Michael Perry used to say that 'it would be wonderful if only Unilever knew what Unilever knows'. Money is spent on academic research to gain insight and wisdom such as 'knowledge that is actually implemented is much more likely to be to be acquired from learning by doing than from learning by reading, listening, or even thinking'.[3]

AFFABILITY

The word affable is derived from the French *affabilis*. The dictionary defines an affable person as one who is 'easy to speak to, pleasant, friendly, and courteous especially to inferiors.'

The word manager is derived from Latin (*manus*) and Italian (*maneggio*). The dictionary defines the word thus, 'to wield, to conduct, to control, to train by exercise, as a horse'.

If you take these meanings too literally, the concept of an

affable manager is an oxymoron. It might appear that no efficient and effective manager can qualify as an affable manager. It is in the nature of his or her work that a manager has to overcome obstacles, which means to convince, cajole, coerce and, if needed, even crucify people into doing things and to coordinate all those actions into a targeted end-result.

That is why Affability is a skill to be learnt, practised and perfected.

- How can you disagree without being disagreeable?
- How can you separate your rival's views from your feelings for your rival?
- How can you listen carefully with an open mind and yet be focused and single-minded?

And yet all these, and more, constitute what is regarded as an affable manager. Recall the story of Arup in Chapter 1 where he displayed the skill of being affable, while not fully respecting the intellect of some of his superiors. When he ran his own factory for the first time in his career, he just had to befriend the local government officers, some of whom did not quite match up to his intellectual abilities. Yet he had to get work done through them by being affable.

People like to communicate and that means not just the opportunity to speak but the right to be heard and in a genuine way. The cause of much strife in the world arises from the inability of people to listen to each other. Even in psychological counselling, practitioners have pointed out the therapeutic effects of just listening to people who want to get things off their chest.

This therefore constitutes a distinctive quality of the affable manager: he or she has to learn to be a good listener. If you look through the training courses run for managers, you will find programs on Communication Skills, Making Effective Presentations and Persuasion Skills but very rarely will you find one on Listening Skills.

Listening is very difficult, especially for managers with authority and a ready audience within their departments or companies. My previous chairman at Hindustan Unilever, the late Prakash Tandon, would exhort trainees to 'listen four times as much as you speak because the surface area of the two ears is four times as much as the lip'. This sounded very appropriate, and I remember the advice to this day. But I have spent a lifetime trying to understand how to do so. I finally found the answer in the research findings of a counsellor and teacher of hearing-challenged people[4] (see Box 3.3).

BOX 3.3

Careful listening: the need for self-training

It is remarkable that we are never taught how to breathe or how to listen. Certainly with respect to breathing, there is more and more awareness of lessons on how to breathe properly. With respect to listening, the lessons are few and far between.

The human ear is a strange product of evolution. It is designed to listen well. In practice, perhaps we do not do it too well.

In reptiles, the two-part ear, comprising the inner and outer ear, is attached to the jaw. Therefore when a lizard eats, it cannot speak or hear. So also conversely. Mammals have a three-part ear, an evolutionary innovation. There is an additional middle ear, which is detached from the jaw.

The mammalian ear is a master of detecting very quiet sounds. Yet we humans do not listen too well. Husbands do not listen well to wives, bosses do not listen too well to employees, and parents do not listen too well to their next-gen children.

Yet listening well and reflecting upon what we have listened to is a key part of implicit feedback. How can we listen better? Strangely it seems that the deaf can teach us how to listen better.[5]

Bruno Kahne is a consultant. He has worked with deaf people, who use sign language to 'listen', as communication consultants for his corporate clients. He has learnt five lessons. The *first* is to look at the speaker in the eye to ensure we are fully engaged and that we can absorb and retain more. The *second* is to avoid interrupting the speaker and to be disciplined to speak one by one. According to Kahne, a group can reach faster results in this way. The *third* is to adopt a simple style of communication rather than a flowery or pedantic style. It is good to be economical with words. The *fourth* is to ask for repetition if the message is unclear. The *fifth* and last lesson is to be focussed on the interaction and to avoid being distracted—with cellphones and Blackberry, for example!

THE 4 As | 51

ADVOCACY

Advocacy is a word derived from the Latin *advocatus,* which means 'the function of pleading the cause of another, the act of urging something'. The dictionary meaning suggests that it is about persuading without power. Management, on the other hand, is associated with direction, hierarchy and power. So where is the connection with advocacy?

In the early stages of one's career, you are the recipient of instructions and the effects of power. You accept them by adapting. You realize that the boss expects you to exercise your leadership on the people who report to you and make sure that things get done. In the middle management phase, you find the need to influence people without their directly reporting to you. In the senior and leadership roles, you may exercise no control over the people you need to influence. This is the manner in which your skills of advocacy develop.

Recall the experience of Arup in Chapter 1. He got his first taste of advocacy when he became the head of a faraway factory. He had to influence juniors, peers and seniors at the head office. He also had to influence external people who could impact his factory: officers in the police, the local administration and the policy makers in government.

When he became CEO, he had to meet ministers and political level people. It was vital for the future of the company that he succeed in persuading them that the policies implemented were killing his company, and with it, the employment of his workers. He had to appeal to their rationality and emotions to get them to do whatever rescue acts were involved. These are the elements of advocacy.

AUTHENTICITY

The final attribute is Authenticity. This is probably the most difficult attribute to learn and practise. It is easier to recognize its absence in an unauthentic person than it is to define what exactly authenticity is. In this respect, authenticity is very much like beauty and character. In most societies, people are likely to consider politicians unauthentic, more so than say teachers, doctors and managers.

What is authenticity? It is being who you are. Your colleagues and peers see you as you are, not the way you would like to be seen. It is their perception of who you are and what you stand for that produces their followership. Followership is used here not in a hierarchical but in an egalitarian sense. It is the voluntary desire or inclination among followers to follow a person, emotionally and physically. Unauthentic people can get others to follow by asymmetry of power, by threat or by coercion. These are not likely to be long lasting.

Genuine followership comes as a result of the person appearing authentic. At a junior career level, there are not many who are following you. So the lack of authenticity may not produce palpable effects. You may not suffer much from its absence in terms of work leadership. But as you move up, the role of authenticity increases in its importance and role as illustrated in Box 2.3 in the previous chapter.

There can be a view that the attribute of authenticity is a consequence of your behaviour and your beliefs. It is not a skill or art that can be learnt. But it is surely helpful to understand the principles that help to build enduring authenticity.[6] Authentic people

- Are cast from the crucible of their sufferings
- Are moulded through formal and informal mentors

- Are those who try to live out a selfless character
- Have a sense that they are called to lead
- Handle privilege with great care
- Are tenaciously focused on their goals
- Invest in the lives of those who follow them

We live in an age when there is a tendency to dismiss character, selflessness and servant-hood as weak and limiting. On the contrary, the attribute of authenticity has become the supreme requirement of modern times. Authenticity arises from your sharing your humanity with those who have chosen to follow you.

Box 3.4 carries a set of words or bullet points which exemplify the 4 As. In the anecdotes that follow, these bullet points form a useful guide.

BOX 3.4: THE MANIFESTATION OF THE 4 As

Accomplishment	**Affability**
Task orientation	*Common sense*
Discipline	*Accommodation*
Learning	*Listening*
Positivity	*Deserving before desiring*
Advocacy	**Authenticity**
Thought	*Integrity*
Creativity	*Trust*
Engagement	*Loyalty*
Communication	*Humility*

ACCOMPLISHMENT

4

DELIVER RESULTS
RELIABLY

I never see what has been done;
I only see what remains to be done.

—Buddha

ENJOY WHAT YOU DO AND
DO WHAT YOU ENJOY

There is a connection between hard work on the one hand
and stress level and success on the other.

You can work very hard and yet not appear to other people
to be stressed. For example, when you are enjoying what you
are doing hugely, or when a musician is on a high or a tennis
player is on a roll. You can also experience the same feeling
when you are totally immersed in the activity and are 'in the
flow', as Mihaly Csikszentmihalyi has pointed out. It is the
'sense of effortless action they feel that tends to occur when a

person's skills are fully involved in overcoming a challenge that is just about manageable'.[1]

People who enjoy their work also feel a better sense of accomplishment and success at work.

In sum, those who enjoy what they are doing do not feel a debilitating stress and also enjoy their success. Enjoyment of work is central to your existence. And it is incredible how many feel trapped in the work that they do.

Your career, indeed your life, has a purpose. When you are working within your purpose, you are happy and have a good chance of 'being in the zone'. You may be aware of your purpose or you may be seeking a purpose. You may be conscious about the purpose or you may be unaware of it.

Through the depiction of a clock face, I have found it easy to see how the harmony between your purpose and your job role contribute to your happiness (see Box 4.1).

The zone between 4 p.m. and 8 p.m. position is highly avoidable. When you are in this zone, you are doing things you hate doing and, to boot, whatever you do makes you feel a lack of self-esteem, that is, you feel unworthy or incompetent.

The zone between 2 p.m. and 4 p.m. is tolerable, but not sustainable. In this zone, you are doing things that you hate but you do them quite well. For example, you may be paid a lot but you do not really enjoy the tasks that you perform. You can do these tasks for some time without becoming unhappy, but not for too long.

So too with the zone between 8 p.m. and 10 p.m. You enjoy the tasks but they do not give you a sense of fulfilment or self-worth. This is quite often connected with a dilemma of the mid-life crisis.

BOX 4.1: THE WAY TO THINK ABOUT PURPOSE

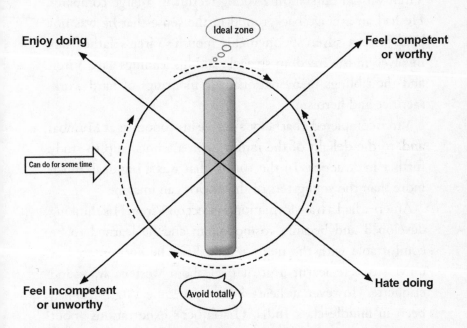

The wonderful place to be in is between 10 p.m. and 2 a.m. on the clock diagram in chart 4.1. This is when you enjoy what you are doing and you derive from your work a great sense of competence and self-esteem.

In fact in a business context, a person in the 10 p.m. to 2 a.m. zone does not appear stressed but may actually cause stress to his colleagues and subordinates! Reflect on Arup's story— Arup seemed to be on top of everything while his colleagues seemed to struggle to retain and learn as much as Arup did.

When you are not in the flow, when you feel a turmoil or conflict, or when the task is beyond your capability or emotional bandwidth, then you feel stress and you show it. It is exactly the opposite of flow as the story of Viren shows.

How Viren's Career Bloomed

Viren was an outstanding young recruit in a large company. He had an average background in the sense that he was not born with a silver spoon in his mouth. Viren's father was involved in the freedom struggle and his leanings gave Viren and the siblings many nationalistic moorings of hard work, sacrifice and heroism.

Viren completed a bachelor's degree in economics at Mumbai and, to the delight of the family, won a scholarship to study further in America. In the 1960s, that was a big deal, much more than the youngsters of the 2000s can imagine.

America had a transformational effect on Viren. His thinking developed and became cosmopolitan and he learned to be comfortable with the many nationalities he encountered at university. He learnt a great deal about western ways and etiquette. However, at heart, he was the same Viren who had been in middle-class India. His father's exhortations about serving the nation in some way, howsoever small, kept ringing in his ears. At a time when migrant Indian students were constantly seeking ways to stay back in the land of dreams, he took a bold and clear-headed decision to return to the socialistic India of the 1960s. Upon return, he joined a values-driven international company.

Viren very quickly became the darling of all his colleagues and bosses. He was thorough in his work, almost studious. According to his seniors, he demonstrated a level of seriousness that was uncommon in his generation. He showed great respect to his bosses and equal courtesy to his peers and juniors. He cared deeply about people and, as a result, he was really loved by everyone he came into contact with in the company. He never tried to show off his somewhat privileged and rare American education.

Such a 'perfect subordinate' had to progress, and very fast at that. Very soon Viren was at the centre of observation by many seniors in the company. He neglected his health due to his growing commitment to his work and family.

His fitness regime got diluted, but he thought that might not matter for a few years; he was still in his thirties. He tended to smoke a tad more than he used to, but, of course, he reasoned that he would give it up as he entered his forties. And so things went on.

He was an intense person and his seniors perceived him that way. Being intense is neither a virtue nor a vice. However, in a business context, when you notice a subordinate who is cut out for big things, a boss realizes that he or she has to balance intensity with a minimum gregariousness. What better way to achieve this than by getting young Viren to lead a regionally dispersed sales team?

Viren travelled a great deal and soon knew his people by name and something about their families, and drove himself as much as he drove them to deliver better sales results. However, there occurred an unexpected downturn in the business. This was not due to market conditions, but due to some prevalent government policies. An unfortunate and accidental fire in his region disrupted his workplace and his schedules.

COPING WITH CONFLICT

The company headquarters decided upon a staff redundancy scheme in his region. Viren was shattered. He did not agree that there was a redundancy issue to be unleashed and he did not agree with the speed with which he was mandated to implement the scheme. He had several discussions with his bosses on the subject but somehow he could not persuade the organization to see it his way. He was frustrated that what he could see and feel was something nobody else could.

He spent long hours with each staff member, sometimes even with the family members. He got totally involved. He felt deeply for each of the staff members who would have to go under the redundancy scheme. The financial rewards of the redundancy scheme were pretty good but that was not the point.

In a frugal, middle-class society, redundancy meant too many negative things. Such events were infrequent enough for society to cast an aspersion on the employee: in economic, social and psychological terms, destroying the self-esteem of the individual. With his staff members' woes, Viren also developed his own mental woes. This caused him considerable emotional stress, sleeplessness and, unfortunately, increased smoking and drinking.

In a few months, Viren was physically, mentally and emotionally sapped. One morning he was found dead in his bed. Yes, dead, without any clear, tell-tale evidence.

It was never clear to me what took Viren: was it suicide, was it an overdose of drinking or sleeping pills? Above all, did the work environment affect him badly enough for his life to be taken? The last question received the same answer from all who knew him. Viren had worked incredibly hard, but equally, got so stressed that his career was cut short: undoubtedly a great loss to his family and the employer.

Here is an anecdote that illustrates how stress causes a perfectly healthy and normal person to behave in a contrarian way. Box 4.2 summarizes the dramatic story of Robert Bales.

BOX 4.2: THE UNUSUAL STORY OF ROBERT BALES

Robert Bales was a well-regarded young man who always seemed to do the right thing. The solid-guy reputation followed him into the US Army Infantry. He earned respect for his quiet maturity and calm after serving in Iraq. On duty in Afghanistan in 2012, Sergeant Bales shot to death 16 Afghan civilians, 9 of them children. Michelle Caddell, who had watched Bales grow up, fought back her tears as she said, 'But that's not our Bobby. Something horrible, horrible had to happen to him.'

Investigations showed that there were a few dark sides to the sergeant—who does not have a dark side? He was once arrested for assault on a woman and had to undergo anger-management counselling. An Army psychiatrist advised that after his multiple deployments and wounds from battle, the sergeant was emblematic of bigger problems: an overstretched military battered by eleven years of combat.

In early March 2012, Sergeant Bales saw a friend lose a leg to a buried mine in Afghanistan. He sent his wife a short message, 'Hard day for the good guys.' One week later Bales walked out of the outpost to the village and shot nineteen people.

YOUR FOUR SELVES

From such incidents, with the passage of time, one might be able to draw some general lesson without reflecting or commenting on the individual concerned. In my experience and view, the short lesson is that the able and upcoming subordinate must learn to manage the four selves that he represents through his work activities. These are the physical self, the psychological self, the ethical self and the spiritual self. I have written about these under the section titled, *The Inner World* in my earlier book.[2]

Fitness is something that a subordinate owes to his boss. The boss has trusted the subordinate to take enough care of his own body so well that the boss can entrust him or her with a few more things to take care of. You should not let your boss down on this count. It is an unwritten contract.

It is pleasing to see health-conscious executives exercising and keeping fit. A management career is extremely stressful, and every young executive should work at managing that stress. Some are unlucky because they develop health problems without bringing it upon themselves. But others squander away their good health on the grounds that office work is stressful. Healthy and young people need not develop stressful social habits, deluding themselves that it is relaxing. Such a hectic lifestyle catches up after ten years.

The second aspect of the physical self is to get enough sleep. Sleep helps you to connect the dots of unconnected information. This is used for creative problem solving in what Gardner refers to as the creating mind. This is what leads to the common expression, 'Let me sleep over this matter tonight.'

When you are in need of sleep, your skills start to decline. Both visual discrimination and memory slide, as also your concentration.

The psychological self is a delicate self. It has all the influences of your deepest emotions, insecurities, ambitions and flights of fancy. These are inherently stressful. So what can you do about these if they are present and are influencing your mind? You cannot wish them away, so you learn how to manage them. 'Every now and then, take a little relaxation, because when you come back to work, your judgment will be surer. To remain constantly at work will cause you to lose your power of judgment,' advised Leonardo da Vinci. So many executives fail to take this elementary action.

George Vaillant undertook the famous Grant Study of 240 high-performing Harvard students over several decades. His findings appear ever so simple, yet day after day, year after year, many perfectly intelligent corporate executives fail to follow the prescriptions.

Vaillant writes about the power of relationships. Warm connections are necessary—from parents, wife, siblings, friends, mentors. Of the men who were thriving at the age of sixty-five, 93 per cent had been close to a brother, sister or cousin. 'The only thing that really matters in life is your relationship with other people,' Vaillant says.

The five factors for aging healthily and in good psychological state as identified in the study are a good education, avoidance of smoking and abuse of alcohol, having good exercise and keeping correct weight. You may wonder whether you need a study over decades to establish these simple truths. You do. The message is worth testing, proving, emphasizing repeatedly for managers never seem to practise what they know.

And you know that these are central to being a good subordinate. If you cannot serve as a good subordinate, you may never reach the role of the CEO!

SINGLE-MINDEDNESS WITHOUT TALKING DOWN TO OTHERS

The more single-minded you are about completing a task well and on time, the more likely it is that you can upset people while you attempt to do so. You can upset others by appearing to be rude, impatient, bossy, unreasonable, pretentious, and a whole host of other unimaginable adjectives. Why would you come through in such ways?

It is likely that others have a different priority of tasks, a different perspective of urgency, or a different mindset at the time your path crosses theirs. Hence a conflict is built into the situation. Your CEO surely values your getting things done in time and in an efficient way, but for sure, he would not want to receive complaints about your brashness or rudeness. In other words, he wants you to get things done but without having to hear anything negative about how you got it done. While getting his or her job done, step on others' toes if you must, but do not take the shine off others' boots. So how do you get the right balance?

The first and most important thing is to recognize and accept the likelihood that you might upset others and the reason is more likely that you are in a hurry than that they are unconcerned, lazy or lethargic. Any shortfall in others' responses should not be attributed to their resistance but to your overbearing sense of priority and urgency.

The second rule is to talk things over so that others in your flight path of completing the task understand why you regard the action as more urgent than they might. In this way they must be persuaded to accelerate their urgency but you too should be willing to slightly let up on your sense of urgency.

The third and last rule is to avoid treating the others or talking to them as though they are hell bent on blocking or obstructing you. This kind of behaviour invariably upsets others. At an extreme level, others may complain to your boss about your style, arrogance and behaviour—and bosses do not like to engage on such subjects.

How Rahul's Accomplishments Were Diluted by His Behaviour

Rahul was an experienced, mid-level general manager in a chemical company. He was quite an accomplished technologist, and was forever bubbling with entrepreneurial ideas of expanding the business with new molecules and new ideas. He would get frustrated that his colleagues and the leaders were not as responsive as he would have liked. New molecules were taking too much time and money to develop, and the corresponding uncertainty in the results was also beginning to show.

Finally Rahul felt he had to move on. His new employer offered him the position of vice president with the independent mandate to bring new molecules to the market. Rahul was greatly excited for two reasons: his long-felt ambition to be a vice president was going to be fulfilled and he now had independent charge to drive the activity.

The new company was a much bigger and more diversified one. Rahul's 'New Chemicals Division' was a start-up division, unfamiliar to the existing managers in the company. In short, Rahul was just another vice president to the existing employees, whereas he thought he was very special.

Rahul was very respectful to the company presidents and

directors who were all his seniors. He valued the strategic perspective involved in his recruitment and was quite kicked about his mandate within the company. He was equally conscious that he had joined as a senior officer. He wore it on his sleeve while dealing with peers and lower level staff. In fact, the lower the level of the staff, the more important it seemed for Rahul to show how senior he was, that he was a 'two star general', not just another officer!

SMALL THINGS APPEARED BIG

The speed with which he would be given the gate pass at the head office, the smile with which juniors would greet him, the promptness with which his requests would be responded to— all these were measures of others' recognition of his importance and seniority. It seems strange, but it is amazing how much such things matter to some people. Business executives tend to be vain and pompous at times, without fully realizing that they are so.

On one occasion he told the security staff at the head office in quite an imperious tone, 'Do you know who I am? You should not keep me waiting more than two minutes. Why don't you keep the gate pass ready for me?'

On another occasion, he admonished the HR departmental head with the remark, 'You know I am not used to such tardiness. In my old company, the HR department dared not take so much time to do such simple things as you people take.'

Within his own department also, he acquired the reputation of being a bully. He treated his project manager as though he were retarding the project rather than advancing it. 'I do not care how you get things done, I demand results, not excuses,' he thundered.

These were not isolated incidents. They seemed to occur with a pattern. The administrative matters were too small to be raised with his peers and bosses. So Rahul did not make an issue of these self-created obstacles he was facing. On the other hand, the unfortunate consequence of his behaviour was that people got offended and took even more time than they might otherwise have taken. Their attitude was, who does he think he is? Rahul got bogged down with small, administrative obstacles rather than getting on with achieving the bigger goals he had contemplated when he joined.

It did not take much time for slippages in the work plan to surface and get noticed by the top leadership. And this is an important point to note. So long as the targets set by the CEO are being accomplished and expectations are being met, being a workplace bully may temporarily not be a great hindrance. Recall the story of Arup and how he could get away with it. If you just have to be a bully, then do only so much that your work expectations are not affected!

But Rahul suffered work slippages. The top leaders also heard on the grapevine things like, 'Rahul is an arrogant, self-serving busybody who treats every lowly person like dirt.' The leaders were surprised because he was ever so courteous whenever he met the leadership. Gradually it emerged that Rahul was perhaps one of those 'kiss up and kick down' managers. When the slippages started to appear, Rahul started to mention how uncooperative people around were. This did not help matters and things then started deteriorating rapidly.

The situation caused the office people to pass around a joke (see Box 4.3).

BOX 4.3

A wealthy American tycoon at the airport repeatedly admonished the porter for various imaginary shortcomings. The black porter bore all the insults calmly, checked in the baggage of his client and withdrew quietly from the check-in counter to the amazement of some watching colleagues. 'Why did you put up with this nonsense?' his colleagues asked him later. 'No problem, mate. I checked him to Chicago O'Hare but his bags to Tampa Florida,' replied the black porter laconically.

Rahul had to leave the new company after some time. So far as the directors were concerned, it was because he had not delivered. So far as the juniors were concerned, it was because he was pompous and deserved to be fired. So far as he was concerned, the organization was not serious about introducing the new molecules, just as he had said of his old company.

The plain fact was that Rahul had not learnt to be a good subordinate before asserting his leadership in the new company. When you switch jobs mid-career, your designation matters less than you think and the new relationships that you build matter more than you think.

How Change Was Retarded at Pfizer

The story of organizational change and chaos in Pfizer Inc after 2000 has been placed in the public domain.[3] Jeff Kindler, a relative newcomer to Pfizer, had been appointed CEO in

2006. He had been chosen from a list of aspiring lifetime Pfizer leaders. His mandate was to change and transform. He recruited from the outside an HR chief called Mary McLeod in 2007 to assist him in his transformational task. She had developed her career as an HR professional in GE Capital, Cisco and Charles Schwab before she joined Pfizer. McLeod was a no-nonsense kind of person, but quite inappropriately for an HR chief, she made the mistake of being unapproachable, preferring to communicate by e-mail and formal meetings. She made her principal preoccupation as 'the care and feeding of the CEO'. Mary McLeod seemed to be delivering what her boss wanted. She became her boss's protector and surrogate while publicly denigrating her own employees. Many unsavoury events occurred over the next three years. Late in 2010, in a 360 degree feedback, more than a third of McLeod's subordinates rated her performance at 1 or 2 on a 5-point scale. Things started to slide and by the end of 2010, she was out of the company.

Author Gurcharan Das has observed, 'An individual who maximizes his friendships and minimizes his antagonisms has an evolutionary advantage, and selection should favour those characters that promote the optimization of personal relationships.'[4]

The lesson from anecdotes narrated in this chapter is that you have to be a disciplined and efficient subordinate, but not an extra-territorial and obsequious subordinate. Pretty simple, but why do so many smart people forget it?

5

OFFER SOLUTIONS

Most people spend more time and energy going around problems
than in trying to solve them.

—Henry Ford

I n this chapter you will explore two dilemmas through
some anecdotes. One is about how to express a difference
of opinion without appearing petulant and dogmatic, the other
is how to use your creativity and innovation at an acceptable
level without slowing down the workplace system.

DEBATE VERSUS QUESTIONING

One great dilemma that every subordinate faces is how to
balance questioning of decisions with accepting and executing.
If you do not agree with the solution emerging out of the
debate on some issue, you feel the need to speak up. If you
persist too much with speaking up, you may be seen as
argumentative and blocking execution. In short, every CEO
or boss has a finite appetite for discussion and debate.

In general, every organization has ambiguous codes about when it is time for debate and when it is time for execution. Nobody tells you which code is operative. The subordinate has to figure it out and act according to his or her judgment. This makes it tricky.

Why Shobha Was Seen as Obstructive

Shobha was the head of a business unit which had three factories and a national sales organization. She had been a company insider for many years. She was obviously well regarded as she had progressed quite far to be the head of a strategic business unit. She was a low-profile leader, solid and well spoken, and a great company loyalist. Her business unit was considered reliable in delivery of sales and profits. Late in her career, a senior colleague was appointed as the new CEO. The CEO was a suave insider who, despite his external conviviality, was known to be a dominating and egoistic leader. Most insiders like Shobha thought that they 'knew him well'. But people who become CEOs may change—it is good to remember that.

Shobha began to have differences with her CEO on one matter: the closure of one of her factories. Shobha could feel it in her bones and also had solid analytics that the factory was uncompetitive and it would take too much money and effort to revive it. The factory had served the company well over many decades. The employees could be well taken care of through a generous separation scheme. Shobha had been advocating a planned closure for several months. The CEO had worked in that factory several years earlier and perhaps had an emotional connect with the factory. He would always ask for another re-think and review. This ding-dong went on for at least three years.

So far as Shobha was concerned, the subject was held in a 'discussion and debate' mode. So she persisted with her view and patiently presented the analysis from different perspectives. But at some stage, the CEO switched to a 'decide and execute' mode. The trouble was that he never made it clear. And as Shobha would later recount, although she knew her boss over so many years, she just failed to read his non-verbal language. The debate carried on when the time had come for decision making and execution..

DEBATING TIME TO EXECUTION TIME

One day the annual budgets were being discussed. The head office, Shobha, her direct reports and the functional heads were all present as always to discuss the budget. Suddenly, the CEO popped the question at the meeting: What should be the future of the factory? The question was posed to every person at the meeting by going around the table. The atmosphere was such that all the people around the table instinctively knew the answer that the CEO wanted. So each person stated his or her view in favour of retaining the factory, some vociferous in their affirmation, and some others rather mutedly. Shobha also could feel that the CEO wanted a particular answer. She was caught in a dilemma. Should she express her genuine view as she always had or fall in line?

Since she had served a long time in the company, she decided to state her view in favour of the factory closure. She did so with all the civility and politeness she could muster. The CEO somehow took it as 'not falling in line'. Here was the whole team wanting to do it in a particular way and Shobha was being obstreperous. How could she?

The CEO asked to see Shobha later on and expressed his inability to continue working with her. He felt her behaviour had bordered on being insubordinate. Shobha was a proud professional. She argued that if the CEO wanted to, he could take the decision and, as a loyalist, she would surely implement it. He feared that she would not execute the decision diligently if she felt quite so strongly about it.

Their relationship and communication had broken down. Shobha agreed to move on. She was leaving a company which she had joined as a young college graduate. Everyone in the company felt that the poor chemistry between two leaders and the ego of the CEO had resulted in the loss of Shobha, a greatly respected and accomplished leader of the company. Too bad.

Several months later, after Shobha departed, the factory did close down! From outside, Shobha felt vindicated, but what was the use?

PRASHANT SUGGESTED THE ALTERNATIVE BUT FINALLY BACKED DOWN

I can think of another situation where the denouement of the story was different. CFO Prashant and Bhushan, his CEO, were locked in a discussion about whether or not to extend more credit to a new distributor, based on the recommendation of the General Sales Manager (GSM). The company had a clearly laid out policy with regard to extension of credit. The policy was based on the usual parameters of the length of the relationship with the company, the track record of payments, and the assessment of credit worthiness. Based on these parameters, the new distributor had already breached the limits. The GSM was pressing for an exception to be made in order to secure a large and prestigious order. Prashant expressed his opposing view, based on his functional professionalism as well as instinct, which was to avoid the risk of extending the credit. He had not been presented any new data which called for the exception to be made.

The GSM, on the other hand, had spoken offline to the CEO and explained his reasoning. Bhushan was somewhat sympathetic to the GSM's view. Prashant resented this behaviour of talking things over offline and not stating the facts upfront at the formal meeting. But what could he do? Bhushan's mind was focussed on how he could resolve the matter.

At a joint meeting, Bhushan reviewed the whole matter de novo and heard all the arguments. Prashant said that since he did not know of any extenuating circumstances to make the exception, he was not in a position to support the GSM's recommendation. The GSM stated that he had explained the extenuating circumstance to the CEO separately. The CFO should just trust the GSM and the CEO!

Prashant sensed that the issue had moved from the 'debate and discuss' atmosphere to the 'decide and execute' one. So he explained his position politely—that he as the CFO had been given the freedom to express his view and the CEO had fully understood the viewpoint. However, as CFO, Prashant understood that there was room for judgment. If the CEO judged the risk worthwhile, Prashant, as the CFO would go along with the decision. Prashant felt he had expressed his professional view, so had the GSM and so had Bhushan. That brought the discussion to a good conclusion. The company did extend the credit to the distributor.

After two years, it turned out that the debt went sour. But the GSM, the CFO and the CEO were all satisfied that they had resolved the issue professionally. Sometimes, you do take such risks. Luckily the size of the risk was not debilitating to the company.

In the case of Shobha, she stuck to her view, perhaps giving the impression of being rigid. Her disciplined mind repeatedly gave her the same answer, namely, plan the closure of the factory. The CEO may well have had an emotional connect with the factory which made him view the solution in a different way. But there was no evidence of his having breached any limit in terms of the respectful or ethical mind. Without any other agenda in play, it would appear that there were two views of the same thing—the half-full and the half-empty view. Shobha's insistence was seen by the CEO as unbending and rigid, bordering on insubordination. Shobha never intended that. The relationship broke down.

In the case of Prashant also, his disciplined mind led him to one conclusion. So did that of the GSM and the CEO Bhushan. Here again there was no disrespectful or unethical angle to the viewpoints. Prashant stated his difference, but with the caveat that there was indeed room for judgment. In this way, Prashant must have come through as flexible and not rigid. The relationship was salvaged.

In short, the way in which you frame your view and the manner in which you express it does matter.

BEING ACCEPTABLY CREATIVE

In solving departmental and company problems, innovative thinking and creativity are usually helpful. But can you be unacceptably creative? Yes, you can. Every organization can handle a certain level and way of being creative.

Creativity means questioning the obvious and the well accepted. Creativity means being a little unpredictable; it means thinking out of the box and disrupting the stability. Creative people are associated with a little eccentricity and craziness.

Solidness means stability. It means accepting much of the tradition and the well accepted. Solid people are associated with predictability and stability. Those you consider solid are not supposed to be eccentric or crazy.

When the ideal qualities of a manager are considered, I find that most people include 'creativity' as well as 'solidness and stability'. Think about it. These attributes are opposites. How do you expect a manager to be both? When the subordinate thinks he or she is being creative, the boss may think otherwise. Further, if you are the subordinate, you too are expected to be creative as well as solid and stable. That for sure is a dilemma for the subordinate.

All companies say that they want fresh ideas from their employees. The reality turns out to be somewhat different. A research paper on this subject has been published recently.[1] The researchers were trying to understand whether there is a connection between the traits of creativity and senior leadership. If you wish to grow into top management, the paper warns, do not to be too creative with your business ideas unless you have plenty of charisma to complement your creativity. Strange, isn't it?

The researchers conducted two experiments among people who were regarded as creative. One study group was at a refinery in India. It involved 364 employees whose jobs required them to find innovative solutions. They had to rank their colleagues' creative expressions and their leadership potential.

Another study group was among American undergraduates. Each student had to offer a creative idea and also evaluate the others for their leadership potential. The end point was to assess whether, among the subjects, there was any connection between their image of creativity and their image of leadership.

The findings from the research were that creative types were seen to be just as competent and personable as their peers, but were judged to be less fit as leaders. This was contrary to the dominant model of leadership that is supposed to encourage useful, non-creative solutions. The researchers also found that creative employees are filtered out on their way up the corporate ladder.

This finding challenges our mental archetype about creativity and leadership. So it appears that stakeholders want leaders who foster a stable and secure environment. However, the research found that creative people can be leaders provided they are also charismatic.

IRFAN WAS DIFFERENT, BUT HOW WAS HE TO SURVIVE?

Irfan joined a consumer-oriented company as a young marketer. He was thought to be an out-of-the-box thinker by the panel that interviewed him. The interview panel discussed among themselves their perception that the company had become too straitjacketed and conventional, that the company's recruitment process rejected any candidate with an innovative mindset. Here was a chance to inject an innovative youngster and they all felt that the recruitment process should bring in more such managers. He was a graduate with a couple of years' work experience in small companies. Irfan's academic credentials were not of the B School-gold-medallist variety. Such types were, however, the company's standard hunting targets. So this would be quite a test for both the company as well as for Irfan.

The company's first year of training involved much routine activity in order to help trainees understand the operations from the grassroots level, namely, stints with the sales force in the market, at the factory with production planning and purchasing and in the depots involved with the distribution of the company's products. Irfan spent the first year of his training in what was appraised as 'a desultory manner'. By nature Irfan was prone to get tired of routine. He was inspired by the unusual. One year of routine seemed interminably boring and long to him.

From his personal viewpoint, Irfan made a very serious attempt to take interest in the day-to-day activities, to be curious and to be diligent. His body language, however, was not in his consciousness. He was unaware that the body language was one of lack of interest. The result was that despite his best attempt, he came through to his bosses as casual and supercilious. Irfan was totally unaware of the negative impression he was creating. About the time he was to be confirmed, he was given feedback in one of his appraisal meetings. He was quite shocked and distressed. Worse still, his probation was extended so that 'he would get one more chance' to establish his worth!

The CEO felt that Irfan might need a special and nurturing boss, so he selected Nehal, a successful and sensitive upcoming leader, to mentor Irfan. Under Nehal's tutelage, Irfan found comfort and guidance. Nehal found Irfan's lateral ideas very interesting and always spoke highly about Irfan to his circle of peers. In due course, Irfan got confirmed and continued to work under Nehal.

Some years later, as part of the company's career planning, it was time for Nehal to move to another role. Irfan could not move with him and, anyway, that would not be proper for Irfan's development. So Irfan got a new boss to whom Nehal explained the whole background. The new boss made a genuine attempt to continue to nurture Irfan.

Like most successful top leaders, the new boss was a left-brained, linear-thinking logic person. Irfan was a right-brained, circular thinking and intuitive person. The new boss did not think particularly highly of Irfan and his informal appraisal began to show in their relationship as well as the output of Irfan at work. So far as Irfan was concerned, Nehal was an angel and the new boss was 'unreasonable'. In fact, Irfan did not consider it his problem at all—after all, Nehal had appraised Irfan to be excellent, had he not? Irfan felt that the whole problem lay with the new boss.

In 1980, two Harvard professors had authored an article in the *Harvard Business Review*.[2] They explained that their title, 'Managing Your Boss', was not very elegant but they had used the term to mean the 'process of consciously working with your superior to obtain the best possible results for you, the boss and the company'. They argued that a subordinate would be making a mistake not to recognize (a) that managing the boss is part of the job role and (b) that the relationship with the boss involved a mutual dependence between two fallible human beings. Hence if you are a subordinate, you must invest the time and intellect to understand the boss, understand yourself, and based on these two bits of data, you must develop and maintain a relationship that fits both.

Irfan, of course, was unaware of this piece of research; to be honest, he fundamentally did not even think that way, nor did he accept its validity. Had he done so, the outcome of his career in the situation described might well have been different.

His new boss progressively downgraded Irfan's performance. From Nehal's view that Irfan was a very bright and innovative manager, Irfan became 'an average manager, a dreamer and not a doer' within two years. From then on, it was a gentle slide downhill until Irfan left the company. He could not help feeling that the company did not really want creative managers and that the leaders only paid lip service to creativity. The company admitted that Irfan was indeed creative but his future as a leader was highly suspect. Since he could not have a career based only on his creativity, they felt it better to let go of his services.

Irfan was creative but thought of as zany. He was slowing down the system in the opinion of his bosses and expressing his ideas in a counter-productive way. Could he have achieved a different outcome had he reflected on his CEO's requirements and adapted his creativity to function in a positive way? Most certainly, yes.

6

BRINGING DYNAMISM TO WORK

Your work is to discover your work and then with all your heart to give yourself to it . . .

—Buddha

On your way up the corporate ladder, it is obvious that you must be perceived as demonstrating energy and positivity in your approach to work. Demonstrating energy and positivity at work is not a matter of style. Neither do all dynamic-looking, talkative people necessarily have the qualities, nor do seemingly low-key, quiet people lack them. It is worthwhile to recall that CEOs and colleagues recognize the quality and consistency of your energy and attitude through multiple interactions over a long period of time. Does this person have the attitude of *doing* rather than merely *thinking*? Is there a visible passion in the work done? Does he or she persist in the face of obstacles?

83

In this chapter, I will address four subjects: what exactly energy and positivity means, how you can have too much, how you can have too little, how you get the balance.

ENERGY AND POSITIVITY IN THE WORK APPROACH

In Chapter 4, there was reference to the fact that you are comprised of four selves, namely, the physical self, the psychological self, the ethical self and the spiritual self. When your four selves operate in harmony, then energy and positivity are delivered into your work space fully. Like beauty, it is the kind of energy you can feel and recognize but find it difficult to define. As it happens with many basic and subtle aspects of life, the most important things are simple to understand, difficult to remember and almost impossible to practise. So it is with energy and positivity.

People sense your energy and positivity when your habit and behaviour is to take charge and own up as and when issues and problems arise. That is the trait that shows up among your qualities. But you may have too much of the take-charge syndrome or too little of it. For example, in management schools you are trained to have active class participation and to be a member of group discussions. If you are the first to speak and you hog the air time, you receive a poor score. If you are silent and inaudible, then too you are not perceived well. You are trained to reach a balance while being evaluated for class participation.

Therefore, a dilemma arises because the Scylla and Charybdis choice is encountered. How do you demonstrate a balanced level of energy and positivity? From a physiological, psychological and intellectual point of view, balanced people are those who are physically fit, possess an inner self-confidence and trust the quality and limits of their mental capabilities. They figure out what is to be done, try to do it, learn from mistakes and feedback and do it again. If you become a bull-in-a-china shop or a laid-back commentator, then others rate you low on energy and positivity.

SHEILA DISPLAYS TOO MUCH ENERGY

There is a subtle difference between 'taking charge' and 'taking over'. A successful subordinate learns about the difference and how to adapt to the difference. Bosses who tell you to 'take over' do not always mean it, because in their mind, they mean 'take charge'. This happens particularly when the boss states that he or she wants fresh thinking and new ideas to be infused into the business.

Sheila joined her new employer, Elite Mills, after a very successful decade and a half with a great and well-respected company. Elite Mills hired her as General Manager, reporting directly to Rajan, the Divisional President. Because Sheila had pedigree in her educational and professional experience, she was a very desirable candidate for Elite Mills to hire.

Rajan had been in Elite Mills for many years and he knew every bolt and nut in the company. He genuinely wanted to transform his division and had an agenda of change. He wanted a solid and experienced GM who could take charge of the day-to-day operations and also bring in fresh thinking. He had gone to great lengths to explain to Sheila all the ideas relating to his transformational project. In fact it was only because there would be action and dynamism associated with implementing such a plan that Sheila made a job switch.

After Sheila joined, Rajan introduced her around to her colleagues and departments. He took great pains to induct her into the operations. Satisfied that she was reasonably well accepted for who she was and her solid experience, and noting that she was familiar with the operations but not well entrenched, Rajan felt it appropriate to let her spread her wings.

SHEILA 'TAKES OVER' INSTEAD OF 'TAKING CHARGE'

Once Sheila got a clear indication that she was to take charge of day-to-day operations, she did so. She travelled to all the divisional units, conducted communication meetings and engaged quite deeply with the executives. Sheila was smart and quick-thinking, but above all, she was creative in the sense that she was capable of synthesizing ideas from several quarters. She was ready to experiment. She sought the ideas of her colleagues and added her own. She then got ahead with implementation. After all, she had clearly been told by Rajan that she was in charge. Sheila was very good at what Howard Gardner calls 'the synthesizing mind'.

Rajan had many informal lines of communication within the company. There were executives who were lower in the hierarchy but had old and long-standing relationships with Rajan. They would keep feeding information to Rajan about the goings on in the division, including about the new GM, not necessarily to gossip, but by way of information. They had been doing so for many years anyway. This way, Rajan got a pretty good idea of the initiatives and ideas that were driving Sheila's work agenda.

One new idea that Sheila implemented related to achieving better outcomes was through better execution focus. She had observed that the management was more focussed on generating ideas rather than selecting some for efficient execution. She felt that ideation and creativity meant that there should be a proliferation of ideas but thereafter, there should be a disciplined approach to focussing on chosen items. Otherwise innovations would get discussed but not executed. Towards this, she started to change the type of dialogue within the division to focus on a few ideas and do them well.

Unfortunately for her, Rajan was wired in the opposite way. He was not unaware of his own creative mind and he loved to 'shoot the breeze' as often as possible. But more importantly, his brain was wired to conjuring up new ideas for the sake of ideation. He was not wired to dropping ideas easily.

DIFFERENCES CROP UP BETWEEN SHEILA AND HER BOSS

Over the next few months, Rajan and Sheila failed to see things the same way. Rajan increasingly felt that creativity was the core strength of the division and that that trait should not be tampered with. Sheila felt that the ideation should indeed be prolific but that some minimum discipline was required to deliver the fruits of ideation. Interestingly, both Rajan and Sheila thought of their respective approaches as supporting innovation. Yet their methods were quite contrary.

Sheila persisted in implementing her concept because after all, she had been told to 'take over'. However, Rajan had intended that she should 'take charge' and saw a subtle difference between his concept and Sheila's implementation.

To Rajan it would have been ideal if Sheila could assess a situation and consult him before doing things differently. Sheila did not mind consulting Rajan, but to her that was not what a person who had 'taken over' would do routinely.

In this subtle wedge sat the future of their relationship. Sheila was trained to place differences on the table and talk them over. Rajan did not like to confront differences and preferred subtle ways of expressing them. To Sheila's discomfiture, the subject was never openly discussed. The wedge grew bigger and bigger until it became a rift. Rajan was not saying 'No' and Sheila never stopped reading a 'Yes'.

Sheila also was a sensible professional, so she did not precipitate matters. She realized that she had got something wrong, something small but important. So she tried to read Rajan's body language since there was not much verbal expression. Over a period of time, she got it right and a new equilibrium in their relationship developed. However, the relationship was not what it was supposed to be. And the results achieved were not commensurate with the professional capabilities of Rajan and Sheila. In other words, they reached an inefficient equilibrium of under-performance in their work output.

It was important for both of them to listen to their 'respectful brain'. They could sense that they had different concepts and that there might be space for both concepts. In this case, they mutually adapted each other's concepts but the troops down below sensed an estrangement.

When you reflect on this episode, the problem appears to be one where the boss did not quite mean what Sheila understood. Sheila felt let down and so did Rajan. Odd, isn't it?

Leslie Perlow, a professor from Harvard, has researched and

written a book on this subject.[1] Her basic idea is that companies, and indeed all organizations where work gets done, lose a lot of time, emotion and alignment due to silence. People do not express their thoughts and views with openness and clarity. People keep silent when they are asked for their views. Or they assume that their views will be expressed only when they are sought. Or, worse still, they say yes at the meeting while actually holding the opposite view. All of these lead to a huge cost due to misunderstanding.

The situation described between Sheila and Rajan has all these characteristics. Sheila might have felt that Rajan was either feeling insecure with her progress or being fork-tongued, or worst of all, resented her initial success. Rajan may have viewed Sheila as not being consultative, not using his experience to her advantage or, worst of all, trying to upstage him.

SHEILA'S CHOICE BETWEEN SCYLLA AND CHARYBDIS

Clearly, as the boss, Rajan could have done some things. But he did only what he did. Hence, there was only one way to search for a way forward. That is, for the subordinate to adjust to the boss. Sheila should have tried to think diligently through what Rajan's agenda for success was, what Rajan wanted by way of feedback or information and build into her agenda of change all such nuanced requirements. She needed to understand that the onus was on her as the subordinate. No subordinate can work on the assumption that he or she has no responsibility to figure out what the boss's needs are. After all, the boss too can be fragile and imperfect.

Thinking along these lines, Sheila became alert to the difference between the 'take charge' and 'take over' mandates during this part of her career.

SUJIT DISPLAYS TOO LITTLE ENERGY

Sujit was the HR head of his company. He was recruited from outside at this senior level because the company wanted new systems and a modern approach. The company style was to let managers market their ideas, carry colleagues with them and implement the ideas collaboratively. Sujit expected strong and visible CEO support for HR upon his recruitment. He held the view that HR transformation could happen only with visible CEO support. Somewhere in the crevice between these two approaches, Sujit fell in.

Sujit was extremely articulate. He could speak with a lot of style, but heavily laden with jargon. The subject of HR lent itself to jargon. However, over a period of time, his listeners would wonder what the meaning or actionable outcome of Sujit's presentation was.

It took several years before many colleagues started wondering whether the emperor was actually wearing clothes. Delivery and performance were perceived to be lagging and inadequate though the presentations and conceptualization were masterful. Sujit also suffered from an image of being arrogant and inadequate in building any collegial relationships. He was an HR resource, so this was all the more galling to his colleagues.

Sujit was judged to be lacking energy and positivity. It was not physical or a tired look that his mentors were referring to. It was Sujit's consistent lack of delivery and his wonderful mastery of words to explain this lapse. When this caper of words had gone on too long, the judgment on Sujit's performance was finally made.

Sujit had to reconsider his future in the company but was quite disturbed by the view that he lacked positivity and energy!

During your career you often encounter situations where you feel uncertain about how to interpret a set of observations.

PERSISTENCE IN THE INDICORP AFFAIR

A consultant or non-executive director can be in this situation. Such a person may feel conflicted about the balance between cooperating with the CEO or/and standing firm with certain principles.

Everyone wants to be known as a manager with principles, a person who stands for right and wrong. Giving in to another view or vacillating is seen as a weakness. And you do not wish to be seen as being vacillating or weak, do you?

But when the roots of the issue lie in the respectful or the ethical mind, the conflict will be greater and more difficult to resolve. In fact, I hold the general view that issues sitting on the respectful and ethical mind petals are the ones where the challenge of 'being practical' to get ahead with it arise.

My friend Gokul had made a senior-level job switch. He had enjoyed a very successful career for twenty-five years in an international company and had joined a senior-level position in an Indian company, let us call it Indicorp (no connection to any real company).

After he joined, he learnt that the CEO of Indicorp had a mixed reputation. He was perceived as successful in running his company and delivering profits. But his directors and seniors were always short on understanding the detailed transactions within the company. The audit committee processes and governance standards in those days were weaker than the standards one encounters these days. Within a year, Gokul became very uncomfortable. He was unsure what exactly he was uncomfortable about. Probably it was the veil around how the company was run and the lack of transparency. But was this Gokul's prejudice or was it real?

A particular M&A transaction was discussed which caused great discomfort to Gokul. The logic of the acquisition was crafted in lofty, strategic terms. In the depths of his heart, Gokul had to admit that he did not understand the mumbo-jumbo. The transaction was between two related parties and the up-to-date, audited accounts of the acquired company were not readily available. The numbers presented were 'generally okay'. The directors had approved the transaction as they felt that the CEO must be trusted. Gokul was the subordinate. How could he resolve it?

It bothered him severely because the conflict arose in his ethical mind. It was a dilemma of right versus wrong, not right versus right. Gokul responded to his instinct and decided he would not be 'practical' about it. He was not willing to get stressed and let the event drain him emotionally.

To cut a long story short, in a well-planned set of moves, Gokul travelled to the acquired company to see how things on the ground were. In the process, as he had hoped, he stumbled on to some inconsistencies. This observation further strengthened his resolve that this was no case to 'be practical'. He systematically collected the documents relating to the inconsistencies. In a bold move, he sought an appointment with the board chairman and thus went above his CEO.

The board was shocked to learn of the likely misdemeanours of the CEO and they did what they had to. Gokul felt vindicated that he had been true to himself. Above all, the energy and positivity with which Gokul did something about his concerns impressed his new employer.

AFFABILITY

7

How to Balance Self-Interest with the Company's Interest

Whatever we treasure for ourselves separates us from others;
our possessions are our limitations.

—Rabindranath Tagore

It is in human nature to think of the self before anything. Self-interest is not a vice. Only when self-interest mutates to selfishness does it begin to be a vice. When you try to maximize your interest with inadequate weight given to the organizational interest, then you may be viewed as bordering on being selfish.

Think of it in another way. Place selfishness at one end of a straight line and selflessness (embodied in Mother Teresa or Mahatma Gandhi) at the other end. The vast middle space in-between can be considered as the zone of self-interest.

When you work in an institution or company, leaders often exhort you to place your organization's interest ahead of yours. This does not mean that you should sacrifice your self-interest. Your CEO or leader is merely requesting you not to maximize your self-interest, but to balance the priority of interests between the organization and yourself. I call this enlightened self-interest.

Here is the story of Shernaz.

THE ANGER AND DILEMMA OF SHERNAZ

I knew Shernaz, who worked in a finance company. She came from a middle-class background and had toiled to qualify as a company secretary. Through sheer dint of hard work in her firm, she had risen over twenty years to become the head of the department. She was known to be sincere and straightforward.

One day a scam was uncovered in her company. The centre of the scam was the CEO himself. He had systematically lied, revealed partial facts, doctored papers and pushed things under the carpet by bullying his senior team into silence. When the board discovered that it had been hoodwinked, the directors felt compromised. Among the many forms of control risks that a company identifies, the most lethal is when the CEO and CFO plot to loot the company. The directors were unaware about the true state of affairs in the company until the scam broke and felt hurt about the deceit. During the investigations, the role of the senior managers in 'not speaking up' was probed. This probe included the company secretary. Were these senior officers silent? Negligent? Or complicit? Based on the available facts, the board decided to fire the top team, including the company secretary.

Shernaz was shattered. She was not an operating officer. She was just handling the secretarial function. How could she be held responsible for the shenanigans of the CEO? How could she speak up under the reign of terror unleashed by the CEO? Why was she among those being fired? She could think of a few others who deserved to be fired but had escaped. She was tormented by the idea that in her social circles, she would be perceived as having been fired for personal impropriety. She was distressed and came to talk to me.

She was angry, really angry. She raved and ranted. She said that it was the most ridiculous and unfair decision on the part of the board. Did the directors not have any sense of discernment or propriety? She too could reveal a lot about the company and embarrass the board and the owners. Should she?

I understood her anger and anguish. After she had settled down, I asked her to consider where her enlightened self-interest lay. It seemed to me that her intention was to hurt the company's reputation since the company was about to tarnish hers. I asked her, what would people think? Would she be seen as throwing mud after being embroiled in the matter? Why had she not spoken up earlier?

She calmed down. Sometimes we try to solve one problem but in the process, we unintentionally create another one. In this case she understood that by reacting to one situation, she would create a new situation which might be uglier. Her sense of enlightened self-interest required her to reconsider her proposed action. Finally, she decided to depart quietly from the company.

Balancing the priority of interests requires you to do something different from your first instinct. It is not easy; it is like pushing water uphill. It does not come to most of us naturally.

DIFFERENT RESPONSES TO A SIMILAR ISSUE

The former Tata Consultancy CEO S. Ramadorai narrates an incident about his early childhood and birthday record.[1] He states: 'I was born on 6 October, 1945 (my parents pretended I was born . . . in 1944, so I could go to school a year earlier since I was too mischievous to be kept at home).'

During his whole career in TCS, nobody knew about this discrepancy and he retired as though he was indeed born in 1944. Had he not narrated this story in his book, the matter of his birthday would be unknown in the public domain.

At about the same time as Ramadorai's book was published, an unfortunate controversy played out in the public domain about the date of birth of India's Chief of Army Staff, General V.K. Singh. The controversy was whether his year of birth was 1950 or 1951. The arguments on both sides of the controversy seemed weighty and the subject received huge administrative, judicial and media scrutiny. It would be diversionary and inappropriate for me to evaluate the facts and issues here in this book.

However, of relevance to the subject at hand, many lay people felt that the organizational interest of the Army, which has a fine image in the country, had been tarnished by the controversy. Many felt that the organizational interest had been given a lower priority compared to personal interest. Whatever the General's case might have been, he could not avoid this unfortunate public 'judgment' on his case.

Box 7.1 demonstrates one interesting way used by a former Chairman and Managing Director of Tata Chemicals, Darbari Seth. He wanted the balance of interest to be simple enough for every co-worker to understand.

BOX 7.1

A balance of priorities

The Tata Chemicals factory at Mithapur, Gujarat, has a room called the Dream Room. It houses pictures and artefacts about the evolution of the factory since its inception in the 1930s. Darbari Seth, a former chairman and managing director of the firm, was known to advocate loyalty for and commitment to the company. He combined simplicity in communicating related ideas and policies to employees, both managers and workers.

- I love and respect people and make champions out of them. I use the authority of my influence, and not of power, in dealing with people.
- To me, my country and my people come first and everything I do is driven by this. I have never done, and I will not do, anything which, according to my own light, is not in the interest of my country, no matter which other interest it might serve.
- I am definitely self-reliant. I am fiercely free and fearless. I have never hankered after any office or reward. I have always worked and lived on my own terms. I trust people. I feel humble. I have no greed and, therefore, no fear.
- I am not deterred by adversity or crisis situations which I look upon as new opportunities for further advancement.
- Not a drop of water that falls on Okhamandal should find its way to the sea. If Mithapur gets water to

drink, then so shall every human being and every cattle head in Okhamandal.

- I always want to be at the giving end, never at the receiving end. I give joyfully and I give till it hurts.

One subject that is often discussed in almost every company is the subject of growth and the related philosophy of the company. It was so in Tata Chemicals too. Darbari Seth arranged to display a placard prominently in the Dream Room. This placard states a test about how Tata Chemicals will decide about new investments and determine where organizational interest lies. It requires you to answer three questions:

- Is this project good for the community and country?
- Is it good for Tata shareholders?
- Is there a distinctive way by which Tata can add value?

This is one of the simplest ways I have encountered to depict corporate strategy as well as the balance of stakeholders' interests.

Another case was in the news in 2012 with respect to one Greg Smith and Goldman Sachs. Smith was an MBA from a top school, Stanford, and working as a mid-level executive in the company. He was the head of equity derivatives in Europe. Smith decided to resign from what must have been a plush job in Goldman Sachs after serving the firm for twelve years. But within a few hours of his resignation, the New York Times carried an article by him. Obviously the actions and timings were well planned. In his article, Smith made all sorts of accusations and comments about the work culture at Goldman Sachs which, according to him, was 'not what it was when he joined the firm'. He accused company executives of 'ripping off their clients', of calling clients by derogatory names like muppet, and of encouraging a culture of eroding integrity and humility.

I have no idea whether he was right or wrong. Perhaps he was responding to his conscience. But the dramatic timing and content of his public letter does raise some questions. Was he placing his own interest above that of the organization?

When you read about someone else or witness the events pertaining to someone else, things appear different from when you are the actor in the episode. This is unavoidable. The best thing you can therefore do is to consult another person, a confidant, when you find yourself in a difficult situation.

Two factors that make it difficult to achieve the desired balance between self-interest and organizational interest are worth mentioning here. The first is about a sense of agency and the second is about judging your behavioural impact.

SENSE OF AGENCY

Sense of agency means your acceptance of the responsibility to act and deal with the issues arising from your current situation. To accomplish the desired outcomes, you have to feel you are in control.

Have you seen a colleague who takes over a department and finds many things wrong with it? The person will not miss a chance to crib about how much of a mess has been left behind, how difficult things are and how an unfair task has been left unfinished. Such a person has a low sense of agency as the cause of the problem has been externalized—to the previous incumbent or the market or the competition. The truth is that no amount of disowning will change the reality. You have to own the problem and act to do something. That is the only way to tackle the situation.

If you have a high sense of agency, you will look inwards for explanations. In this way, learning and behavioural change become possible and plausible. You will then behave as though the desired outcome depended on you. For any of us stepping into a new role, you inherit a set of credit notes and debit notes. It is then for you to advance into the future with those credit and debit notes.

A sense of agency helps a great deal to own a situation and advance the organizational interest.

JUDGING YOUR BEHAVIOURAL IMPACT

It is certain that there will always be an asymmetry between your self-image and the image in others' minds. Other people will have a lower, less embellished view of your contributions and skills compared to your opinion about yourself.

All the while that you act and behave as though you are a terrific manager, others are viewing you, not necessarily as a poor manager, but as no great shakes! You act and behave as though the whole department or company centres around your contribution, but others think differently. You think you are very fair and task focussed, while others may see you as unemotional and work-driven. This asymmetry of views makes it very difficult for you to judge the effect of your behaviour on others. Worse, you may think you are a picture of courtesy at work whereas others may perceive you as uncivil at times!

In fact, incivility at work is considered to be increasing and the tests of what is considered incivility seem to be getting more stringent. Academics have been focussing on this subject. Incivility is often a manifestation of the phenomenon of a manager placing his interest above the organization's interest.

INCIVILITY AT WORK

A book has been published recently on the subject of incivility at work.[2] The authors are academics at US business schools and they make startling revelations about incivility, which they define as 'the exchange of seemingly inconsequential inconsiderate words and deeds that violate norms of workplace conduct'.

Of the cases of incivility that their research recorded, 40 per cent were among peers and colleagues; they were not top-down. Half the respondents polled by the authors said that it is not unusual to see employees treat their co-workers badly. According to the authors' research, incivility at work is pervasive and growing.

I was intrigued to learn about this research and what the authors consider as incivility. Incivility is subjective and circumstantial. A joke can be acceptable in one situation but the same joke may not be acceptable in another situation. Just as the British have Irish or Scottish jokes, in India too we have jokes about certain communities. However, we know that under certain situations, such jokes became improper to narrate.

The list of incivilities by the authors includes items such as: interrupting a conversation, talking loudly in common areas, arriving late for a meeting, failing to return a phone call and showing little interest in another person's point of view.

If this list were to be accepted, then I have to admit that I have been uncivil many times! This realization makes me feel bad as I could have hurt someone without meaning to and without knowing that I had hurt that person. I became sensitive and decided to observe matters more closely. Here is what happened the week after I had read the book.

I receive blank appraisal forms each year to fill up for the people who report to me. The forms contain no personal details; they just have the person's name, the department and the dates of birth and joining. I gave the forms to my secretary to send to each person in a sealed envelope with my handwritten instructions of the information that I needed from them. I never thought of my action as uncivil.

One of my reportees told me that she was miffed, because the envelope had been sent with my secretary's handwriting on the envelope. For her the appraisal form was hugely personal and it was not appropriate for my secretary to have handled it. She felt that I should have handed the form in person or sent it in an envelope addressed to her in my hand. I was taken aback. By now I had become sensitized to the idea of incivility and that what had to be dealt with was actually an issue of perception!

INSIGHTS FROM BRAIN SCIENCE

The brain experiences the workplace as a social system. That is why a career is very important to all of us. We spend as much as half of our lives in our professional career.

Neuroscience suggests that physiological changes do happen when a person feels a sense of rejection.[3]

The activity and response of the brain is similar in two very different situations. When you are offered food which you like or dislike, your brain responds in the same way as when you have an interpersonal experience which you like or dislike.

When you are reprimanded, or given an assignment that you perceive as unworthy or given a poor raise, it is the equivalent of being hit on the head. Contrary to popular perception, the brain equates social needs with survival rather than with well-being. You can feel as desperate when you feel socially ostracized or excluded as when you are hungry or physically threatened.

We now know that a bad interpersonal interaction leaves survival-related marks on the brain. No boss would like to inflict such marks on his subordinate. Hence, successful executives should be far more sensitive to the effect of their behaviour on others.

But how can incivility affect our ability to balance our own interest with that of the organization? It does so by producing a short-circuit in the brain. The brain has a part called the amygdala. Instant and emotional responses are triggered in the amygdala. Normally this emotional response is subsequently vetted and processed in the rational part of the brain called the neo-cortex. This is how a reasoned and logical response is formulated by the brain. However, under intense emotional situations, the amygdala hijacks the action response without referring the matter to the logical part called the neo-cortex. All this causes great stress to the individual and his or her judgment gets impaired in balancing the priority.

LEARNING THROUGH MISTAKES

It is not possible to avoid making mistakes. One can only try to reduce the number and the frequency of their occurrence.

Making mistakes in human relations is a characteristic of all leaders. Those around notice these mistakes but do not give any feedback.

It is possible to climb out of a trap when one has inadvertently fallen into it. However, you should first try to avoid falling into these traps. A manager must know and admit that he is in a trap; otherwise there is no chance of his getting out of it. If a trap becomes a permanent one, then leadership capabilities get severely diminished.

Other people's experiences are incredibly valuable. You can see other people's faults easily, and find it very tough to see your own. This is why through anecdotes from other people's careers and experiences, you can recognize situations and relate to them with parallels of your own. Personal learning, thus, can be accelerated by observing and studying others' experiences.

Learning about the impact of your behaviour requires a high level of self-awareness, understanding other people, and getting the best out of relationships and networks. Such expertise is essential for a person to develop and exercise the capability of organizing people around a common goal: inspiring them to work together and achieve certain targeted results by identifying and using opportunities rather than watch opportunities pass by.

MAKING A RISKY CAREER CHOICE

This book is not about established leaders but about the way leaders in the making behave. Such young people need to behave and actually come through as placing the company before self. I narrate the experiences of S. Ramadorai as told by him in his book.

TCS had been set up as a division of Tata Sons in the late 1960s. TCS developed a good business alliance with Burroughs, a big mainframe computer company. The alliance lasted four years during which the business grew very satisfactorily. Burroughs was one of the top three companies in the world in micro-programming and software architecture. In 1977, Tata Sons received an industrial licence to manufacture computer hardware in India. It was very tempting to mitigate the risk and to create a joint venture with Burroughs, who had anyway earlier approached Tata Sons to establish a joint venture in India. The JV would sell Burroughs systems in India and develop software to run on the systems. Tata Burroughs was established in 1978.

This move placed TCS in an awkward position. TCS had two choices—to fold into Tata Burroughs or to strike out on its own by seeking non-Burroughs business. After 'some tense discussions' between F.C. Kohli and Tata Sons, it was decided that TCS would continue as a separate entity. Kohli felt strongly that TCS had a good future on its own rather than merely as an arm of a successful multinational. An independent TCS would behave and act like a start-up whereas the JV would act like an MNC arm. The issue of where Ramadorai would stake his career choice also arose alongside.

As agreed between Tata Sons and Burroughs, twenty-five engineers were offered a transfer to the JV. Ramadorai was one of them. But Ramadorai's own instinct was to stay with TCS. Indeed he felt informally encouraged to stay in TCS by the signals from Kohli. The dilemma was that it was a risky option. Ramadorai writes that he followed his instinct and the interests of TCS and stayed back.

Since India's IT market was not yet ready, business had to

be scouted for overseas. TCS applied to the government for permission to set up an overseas company for this purpose. Miraculously the permission was given. And Kohli asked Ramadorai to shift to the US as the first Resident Manager.

Ramadorai had to weigh the option. Here he was in Mumbai with a young family and all the trappings of middle-class security. He was now required to move with his family to live in the US and develop a business which nobody knew existed. He did so. The rest is history.

Writing about the incident, Ramadorai recalls, 'Why did Kohli choose me? I asked him much later and he said, "There was no one else I could trust." He wanted someone who was willing to take up this immense challenge. He felt I fitted the bill.'

I can recount the experience of my Tata Sons board colleague, R.K. Krishnakumar. In the mid 1990s, he was the CEO of Tata Tea, a prominent company, and well settled in Kolkata. At that time I was the CEO of his competitor company, Brooke Bond Lipton India. During the 1990s, the tea industry in the east went through a harrowing time with kidnappings and death threats from ULFA (United Liberation Front of Asom), an activist organization in Assam. Krishnakumar was in the thick of meeting these challenges. He was the CEO of Tata Tea and also the national president of the tea trade body. In fact one of his own executives, Bordoloi, had been kidnapped. At the same time another incident in Tata triggered a dilemma for Krishnakumar.

In 1997, the Indian Hotel Company (Taj Mahal Hotel) was going through its own leadership convulsions. Chairman Ratan Tata was deeply engaged in sorting out the serious issues that had cropped up in this regard. He desperately needed a new CEO to take up the challenge of putting Indian Hotels back on track. He turned to Krishnakumar, a veteran of the 1963 Tata Administrative Service.

Krishnakumar recalls, 'I knew nothing about the hospitality industry or how to run a hotel. How could I have been of help? But here was my chairman asking me to pitch in. What should I do?'

A general does not choose his battlefield, and he just goes where the call requires him to go. And, literally overnight, Krishnakumar packed his suitcase in Kolkata and arrived in Mumbai to head Indian Hotels. The story of how the issues were resolved and the company recovered its glory has been recounted in the public domain. The focus here is about how organizational interest was placed ahead of personal interest.

THE HIGH MAINTENANCE EXECUTIVE

When an executive frequently places his own interest ahead of the organization, he or she tends to show certain behavioural traits, for example:

- constantly inquiring what is in it for me?
- requiring constant reassurances of being valuable and pep talks
- needing more maintenance time from the bosses
- showing almost an obsession with the career path and direction
- comparing with peers and juniors and asking about why others are progressing better than himself or herself.

These traits add up to what I call a high-maintenance executive. These typically are very bright and competent people but they seem to lack an emotional sensitivity and awareness. They can be hugely exasperating to the CEO. A few get away, but many stumble in the late stages of the career trajectory.

SATISH DHAWAN AND ISRO

Originally known as the Sriharikota Range (SHAR) and later named after a great Indian space scientist, Satish Dhawan, SHAR is India's primary orbital launch site to this day. The first flight-test of Rohini-125, a small sounding rocket, which took place on 9 October 1971, was the first ever spaceflight from SHAR. Since then technical, logistic and administrative infrastructure has been enhanced. Together with the northerly Balasore Rocket Launching Station, the facilities are operated under the ISRO Range Complex (IREX) headquartered at SHAR.

The range became operational when three Rohini-125 sounding rockets were launched on 9 and 10 October 1971. Previously, India used Thumba Equatorial Rocket Launching Station (TERLS), on the west coast of India, to launch sounding rockets. The first test launch of the complete SLV-3 rocket occurred in August 1979 but it was only partially successful following a malfunction in the second-stage guidance system. SHAR facilities worked satisfactorily during the SLV-3 preparation and launch. On 18 July 1980 the SLV-3 successfully launched India's third satellite. Out of the four SLV launches from SHAR, two were successful. The former president of India, A.P.J. Abdul Kalam, has recalled how Satish Dhawan behaved after the first failed launch and then the second successful launch.[4]

It was usual to have the media waiting for a press conference after the launch. At the press conference, the ISRO leadership would comment on the launch and answer questions. When the first mission developed a glitch, Satish Dhawan told his team that he would address the media. He owned up the mistakes as he briefed the press. When the second mission was successful, he requested the team to address the media. In a sense, he wanted them to be seen to be taking the credit.

Serving organizational interest with great commitment can be balanced with your self-interest, you just have to try a little harder.

8

DISAGREE WITHOUT BECOMING DISAGREEABLE

*The people to fear are not those who disagree with you
but those who disagree and are too cowardly to let you know.*

—Napoleon Bonaparte

When I was writing the early draft of this chapter, the content was focussed on encouraging the subordinate to express his or her disagreement: you owe that to your boss. 'Sir, that is very easy to state, but how do you go about it? The office situation can be very daunting to a young person,' posed my young acolyte.

When people live and work together, disagreement is inevitable. Education teaches you to be individualistic, and many societies encourage individualism in thinking and behaviour. Disagreements are not bad, and they are actually the lifeblood of our society and our companies. We would be crippled without diverse views. Clearly, however, it is unacceptable organizational behaviour to express disagreements in a disagreeable way or to wreck the ship of debate by rudeness.

In every company, there is a hierarchy. The question of whether you can disagree with your seniors and, if so, how to express your disagreement is influenced by both the norms of the society you belong to and the way the culture of that company has evolved. In other words, a culture of how disagreement is expressed builds up. I worked in Unilever and in Tata. The way of expressing disagreement in Unilever was far more direct and upfront compared to Tata: it could be the Dutch influence! My purpose is not to compare the two, but my perception required that I adapt rapidly when I changed jobs.

If you are an upcoming subordinate, it is not appropriate to suppress your opinions but you must learn how to express your views and disagreements constructively. It is a very important skill. In Box 8.1 an anecdote is narrated which illustrates this.

BOX 8.1

Hanuman in the court of Ravana

A delightful story from the Ramayana demonstrates that the subject of expressing disagreement agreeably is not a new one. Hanuman, the emissary of Sri Rama, had found Sita in the Ashoka forest in Lanka. He made her the promise of returning soon with Sri Rama to rescue her from her incarceration by the demon king Ravana. Before his return to Sri Rama, Hanuman created considerable havoc in Lanka by burning palaces and attacking guards and warriors. His goal was to be captured and taken to Ravana's court. Once there he could deliver an ultimatum that unless Ravana agreed to free Sita peacefully, there would be war with Sri Rama.

Ravana's eyes rolled in anger at the havoc created in his mighty kingdom. He despatched warrior after warrior to capture or kill Hanuman, and each time he ratcheted up the level of skill and accomplishment of the warrior. But to no avail.

Finally, Hanuman submitted himself to capture and was dragged to Ravana's court. He managed to deliver his message to a furious Ravana. Everyone in the court was baying for Hanuman's life and Ravana had little opposition to the idea that Hanuman must be punished through death.

Ravana had a brother called Vibhishana. He disagreed with the impending decision. According to Vibhishana, the rules of politics and diplomacy were that messengers can be punished, but never killed. But how on earth could he communicate this opposite view in a court which was in a frenzy? He hit upon an idea.

He addressed his brother with sweet words of genuine admiration before recommending a different course of action. 'My brother, you are so learned and the gods have bestowed on you many boons on account of your knowledge and wisdom. You are well aware that there is an accepted rule in politics and diplomacy. Surely a great emperor like you cannot allow your prestige and equity to get diluted by following a path which is not prescribed! My king, it behoves you not to kill the messenger, but to punish him severely. Please consider my suggestion.'

And that was how Hanuman's tail was set on fire as punishment. The story of the Ramayana continued thereon.

In my experience there are several practical types of disagreement. You need not have the same approach to all of them. Those where there is a principle or ethical aspect involved must be dealt with without any ambiguity or sophistry. If you do not deal with such disagreement unequivocally, you will find your position compromised and you will develop internal stresses. However this does not mean that you have to behave disagreeably. The example of Vibhishana dealing with a disagreement of principle in a constructive way illustrates this.

Disagreement requires to be expressed sometimes at an institutional level (a company disagrees with, for example, a current government policy) and, at other times, at an individual level (a manager disagrees with the company leadership's view).

INSTITUTIONAL-LEVEL DISAGREEMENT

Unilever, a global ice cream player, sought to enter the ice cream market in India in the early 1980s through its Indian subsidiary. Unfortunately under the industrial laws at that time manufacture of ice cream was reserved for the small-scale sector; of course it was a highly illogical position but that was the law. Many representations were submitted for a review of the law but to no avail and Unilever had to wait for over fifteen years.

When industrial liberalization began in 1991, the receptivity in the government to market-oriented ideas improved. The business and legal team of Hindustan Unilever found that the definition of ice cream under the food laws mandated the compulsory use of dairy milk fat. Why not substitute the milk fat in the ice cream formulation with vegetable fat? In this way the product would not qualify as an ice cream. The product would be called a 'frozen dessert' and would escape the mischief of reservation for the small-scale sector.

The company had expressed its disagreement to the authorities over the years. Now in the changed atmosphere of the 1990s, it felt it should take a chance to secure early market entry. An informal sounding out of the concerned officers in the government was encouraging. I was the CEO of Brooke Bond Lipton, a subsidiary of Unilever, and the company set up a spanking new factory in Nashik.

This is how the company entered the market. There was some criticism, but the company managed to protect its business interests both from a legal and an ethical perspective. Some years later, of course, the law on reservation changed!

On another occasion, I participated in one company's leadership meeting when a proposal for a business alliance was presented. The proposal had taken into consideration all the relevant aspects of commerce, foreign partnership, and the law as applicable to that business. There was one illogical law, somewhat akin to the ice-cream example, and a way around the problem had been proposed. Some of the members present felt that the bypass solution around the illogical law was in order but that the detail had been inadequately thought through and planned. They expressed their concerns, and they suggested the precise ways in which more robustness could be achieved. The operating team was initially a bit miffed; they had expected a clearance and had planned all the follow through actions. To their credit they went back with the suggestions and reworked their proposal. They secured the unanimous agreement of all the members around the table in due course.

INDIVIDUAL-LEVEL DISAGREEMENT

In any company, after everyone has expressed his or her view, the final decision has to be taken by the boss. The final decision cannot be an average of everyone's opinion; it must be the best and most practical among the opinions heard. That final decision will almost surely be at variance with the individual opinion of every participant. The decision, however, has to be implemented and executed by every individual. How can you implement with your full commitment a decision you do not believe in one hundred per cent? More often than not, you have to and you can.

Girdhar and Harinder worked as colleagues at the head office of the same firm. Girdhar had a background in business development, whereas Harinder was a financial person. They made quite a good team at the head office, where they worked closely with the company CEO. They also got along well at a personal level.

Their firm was implementing a diversification project into a new business. Over the previous few years, the business prospects had been studied carefully, and the plan had been drawn up quite thoughtfully by some bright managers of the company.

A question had arisen about the choice of technology. There were two types of technology available; both were of recent origin and the question was which one to choose. In this narrative, we can refer to them as A-Tech and B-Tech. The CEO took the bold decision that the company would try both by setting up two units, each unit using one technology. It was a little expensive, but it provided valuable exposure to the managers.

After implementing the technology, experience and market response data was available to all concerned equally. The interpretation of the results was very different among the team members and a great debate arose about whether or not there was any difference. What should be the future strategy of the company in this regard?

Both Girdhar and Harinder were in favour of A-Tech, but the CEO was in favour of B-Tech. The CEO had no hidden agenda or personal angle, so it was just a difference of judgment. The CEO was technology-savvy and was influenced by the future advances that B-Tech offered, whereas Girdhar and Harinder were influenced by the market responses to the products produced by the two routes. The general sense that Girdhar and Harinder had was that A-Tech found more favour among the executives involved. But people did not want to speak up. Who was to tell the CEO?

The CEO was annoyed. He was a charismatic leader, a person of few words and believed in giving messages obliquely rather than thump the table to assert his views. How should he handle this situation of the management being in what he called the 'eternal debating mode'?

After considerable thought, the CEO sent out a memo, in which he effectively asserted that the decision of the company was in favour of B-Tech and that it would be inappropriate for managers henceforth to continue debating the choice of technology. The choice had been made. Now get on with it. That was the message.

The reaction to the CEO's decision and subsequent behaviour of Girdhar and Harinder is the real story here. Girdhar felt that the CEO had closed the debate in an uncharacteristically high-handed and undemocratic way. How can such an important decision be taken unilaterally and be closed through an office memo? Girdhar felt that a 'wrong' decision had been taken.

Harinder, on the other hand, felt that it was a close call and someone had to take the final decision, and that it had to be the CEO. At a personal level, he felt that a less preferred option had been selected. But in his mind it was not a choice between right and wrong, but between two potentially right decisions.

Harinder's perspective was quite distinct from Girdhar's. He felt that the choice was between 'right' and 'right', whereas Girdhar felt that the choice was between 'wrong' and 'right'. These are very different perspectives and lead to very different types of behaviour as the rest of this story will demonstrate.

In the review and planning meetings that followed, Girdhar would engage with the operational details, as befitted his background. He took great pains to understand the operations and the people. He read a lot of magazines and attended conferences to enhance his understanding. His questions and type of engagement sometimes came through to the observer as being inquisitorial and detailed. The more he studied and debated, the more he was convinced that the company had arrived at the wrong decision.

Harinder, on the other hand, engaged at the more strategic level and constantly kept an open mind about the developments and their analytics. He was rich in his understanding of the results and asked his questions in a pleasant way. He never came through as being tough, but was seen as curious and sceptical, not aggressive by any means. He too gradually drifted to the view that perhaps the wrong decision had indeed been taken.

The CEO was a sensitive watcher of these dynamics. His own style was to let the management get on with their job. He would question operational performances up to a point, and would express his doubts and discomforts in a somewhat gentle way. However he could observe that Girdhar was rather aggressive in his questioning while Harinder was more circumspect. The CEO interpreted this behaviour to be partly arising out of the intrinsic nature of the individuals. This is something that cannot be helped and each one was being true to who he was.

Over time the CEO became increasingly doubtful about the views of both his colleagues with respect to the choice of technology that he had made. He developed a doubt as to whether Girdhar and Harinder were committed to this major diversification. But both of them behaved with great professional courtesy and loyalty. Neither could be faulted on this count.

After several years, it became obvious to everybody in the company that the choice of B-Tech was incorrect. The company should have taken A-Tech. But much water had flowed under the bridge. The new business was mature and many things required to be done to turn around a not-so-good situation.

Both Girdhar and Harinder had turned out to be right and the CEO was wrong. Girdhar felt convinced that a 'wrong' choice had been made initially, whereas Harinder continued to feel that a 'choice between two right choices' had been made—and that such decisions can go wrong. That is the essential nature of entrepreneurial decisions in business. So what!

This incident concerns a genuine difference about a business issue. Sometimes there arises a difference about the principle or ethics of a particular course of action. In this case, it is inappropriate to suppress the difference and compromise. You cannot live with the decision and you must excuse yourself from the decision explicitly. Some incident or the other usually precipitates the difference.

How Gopi Extricated Himself from the Disagreement

I witnessed the case of Gopi and Kersi. They were both CEOs of two large companies, both owned by the same multinational. The parent wanted to merge the companies to provide a common balance sheet but leaving the autonomy of the two large entities intact. It was to be a financial merger, not an operational merger. Kersi became the boss of the combined company. Very soon he started to merge the operations on the grounds of financial savings. Gopi argued hard against these ideas but to no avail. Since he disagreed with the original principle being back-tracked, Gopi moved on from the company, which he had served long. Unfortunately, Kersi's grandiose ideas of merging operations and other growth initiatives left the company with a poor share price for a decade.

From the public domain, two incidents of disagreement that arose from a principle are summarized in Box 8.2, both of which triggered unintended social revolutions.

BOX 8.2

Rosa Parks

On 1 December 1955, Rosa Parks, a 42-year-old African-American woman who worked as a seamstress, boarded a Montgomery City bus to go home from work. She sat in the middle of the bus, just behind the ten seats reserved for whites. Soon all of the seats in the bus were filled. When a white man entered the bus, the driver (following the standard practice of segregation) insisted that all four blacks sitting just behind the white section give up their seats so that the man could sit there. Mrs Parks quietly refused to give up her seat.

Her action was spontaneous and not premeditated, although her previous civil rights involvement and strong sense of justice were obvious influences. 'When I made that decision,' she said later, 'I knew that I had the strength of my ancestors with me.' 'I'd see the bus pass every day,' she said. 'But to me, that was a way of life; we had no choice but to accept what was the custom. The bus was among the first ways I realized there was a black world and a white world.'

She was arrested and convicted of violating the laws of segregation, known as 'Jim Crow laws'. Mrs Parks appealed her conviction and thus formally challenged the legality of segregation.

The Montgomery Improvement Association, which was composed of local activists and ministers, organized a series of civil actions and boycott. As their leader, they chose a young Baptist minister who was new to Montgomery: Martin Luther King, Jr. Sparked by Mrs Parks' action, the boycott lasted 381 days, into December 1956, when the US Supreme Court ruled that the segregation law was unconstitutional and the Montgomery buses were integrated. The Montgomery Bus Boycott was the beginning of a revolutionary era of non-violent mass protests in support of civil rights in the United States.

Mohamed Bouazizi

Mohamed Bouazizi was born in 1984 to a construction worker in Libya. His father died of a heart attack when Bouazizi was three, and his mother married Bouazizi's uncle some time later. Bouazizi lived in a modest stucco home in a rural Tunisian town burdened by corruption and suffering high unemployment. He was educated in a one-room country school in Sidi Salah, a small village about 19 km from Sidi Bouzid. With his uncle in poor health and unable to work regularly, Bouazizi, who was ten, started working and quit school in his late teens in order to work full-time.

He supported his mother, uncle, and younger siblings, including paying for one of his sisters to attend university, by earning approximately US$140 per month selling produce on the street in Sidi Bouzid. He was also working toward the goal of buying or renting a pickup truck for his work. A close friend of Bouazizi said he 'was a very well-known and popular man [who] would give free fruit and vegetables to very poor families'.

Local police officers had the habit of mistreating vendors, regularly confiscating the small wheelbarrow of produce; but Bouazizi had no other way to make a living, so he continued to work as a street vendor. Around 10 p.m. on 16 December 2010, he had contracted approximately US$200 in debt to buy the produce he was to sell the following day.

On the morning of 17 December, he started his workday at 8 a.m. Just after 10:30 a.m., the police began harassing him again, ostensibly because he did not have a vendor's permit. Street vending in Tunisia, according to the head of Sidi Bouzid's state office for employment and independent work, required no permit.

Bouazizi's family claims he was publicly humiliated when a 45-year-old female municipal official, Faida Hamdi, slapped him in the face, spat at him, confiscated his electronic weighing scales, and tossed aside his produce cart. It was also stated that she made a slur against his deceased father.

Bouazizi, angered by the confrontation, ran to the governor's office to complain and to ask for his scales back. Following the governor's refusal to see or listen to him, even after Bouazizi was quoted as saying 'If you don't see me, I'll burn myself,' he acquired a can of gasoline from a nearby gas station and returned to the governor's office. While standing in the middle of traffic, he shouted 'How do you expect me to make a living?' He then doused and set himself alight with a match at 11:30 a.m. local time, less than an hour after the altercation.

Bouazizi died eighteen days after the immolation, on 4 January 2011. According to Bouazizi's mother, Bouazizi undertook his action because he had been humiliated, not because of the family's poverty. 'It got to him deep inside, it hurt his pride,' she said, referring to the police harassment.

Like Rosa Parks, Bouazizi had learnt to accept illogical laws and the bullying of the local government officers. One day he triggered an event which, unintended by him, led to the Arab Spring movement.

SOME INSIGHTS FROM MY EXPERIENCES

Pick your battles

You do not have to address every injustice or irritation that comes along. Quite often the difference between the opposite views matters less than you think. But it is a mistake to stay silent when an issue matters because the cost of silence can be bitterness, resentment or feeling disconnected.

Understand the stakes

Even if you think that you know the other person's issues, it can't hurt to pose a direct question, 'What's your real concern?' Keep the dialogue on. If you break the dialogue, it takes a lot to get it back on track.

Wait until you're calm

Your arguments must always be on the issues rather than with the person. When emotions run high, disagreements can turn personal, and that's rarely productive. Recognize when emotions are charged, and don't have the conversation until you have a cool head.

Don't terrorize

Try not to go on a lawyer-like attack with a litany of yes-or-no questions. This tack is aggressive, puts the other person on the defensive, and can belittle the person.

Focus on the common interests

Keep the common goal and good in mind. If an argument turns nasty, nobody wins. Tell the person how much he or she means to you and how much you value his or her opinion.

Clear the air rather than win

In many instances, the disagreement will end in détente. Don't try to win the argument; it's more important to focus on understanding why the other person thinks differently.

Consider compromise

It doesn't get you exactly what you want, but it can be an effective way for people to overcome a disagreement and move forward. A compromise doesn't have to be equal to be acceptable.

9

PACKAGE INTELLECT WITH EMOTION

Know thyself

Nothing in excess

—Inscriptions at *Delphi*

Tata old-timers recall an episode when J.R.D. Tata faced an embarrassing complaint from a long-standing shareholder at an annual general meeting. In those days, company AGMs would be long and tiresome for the chairman because the proceedings would be circumlocutory and the way in which many of the shareholders would speak was long-winded. J.R.D. Tata, however, believed that it was the one day in the year when shareholders could meet the directors and ask their questions about the company and its products. Some shareholders may not be precise and to the point, but it is essential for the chairman to be courteous and patient with shareholders and conduct the proceedings with complete sincerity and diplomacy.

In the early 1970s, at the AGM of the Tata Oil Mills Company, TOMCO for short, J.R.D. Tata was in the chair. An elderly shareholder complained on behalf of his wife that there had been an unacceptable deterioration in the quality of the company's soap, Hamam. In those days, soap makers had no access to imported raw materials for soap-making and had to manage by upgrading less-than-ideal local vegetable oils. Consumer quality complaints therefore had increased with respect to the products of TOMCO and its competitors.

JRD explained the facts, apologized, and offered to send the shareholder's wife a dozen cakes of better quality Hamam soaps as free replacement. The shareholder said that his wife would still be dissatisfied. JRD then offered to spend time with the shareholder after the meeting to explain in more detail. The shareholder was still dissatisfied. JRD reluctantly suggested that the wife could switch to a competing product, but still the shareholder was unhappy.

Each time that JRD escalated the palliative measures, the shareholder's response was that his wife would not be satisfied. Finally, with equanimity and a light smile, JRD humorously advised the shareholder to change his wife! The tense atmosphere got defused and the bonhomie of the AGM was re-instated.

The incident illustrates how a logical and well-reasoned approach often gets enhanced with an overtone of emotion, in this case, a sense of humour.

EMOTION EARNS A PERSON LOVE, WHILE INTELLECT EARNS RESPECT

Emotion appeals to the heart of a person. Intelligence appeals to the mind of a person.

From your schooldays right into your career, you feel a pressure to show your peers and bosses how intelligent and clever you are. You want intelligence to be your visiting card. You have been brain-washed to believe that intelligent people advance better in life and in their careers. It is intelligence that the bosses would notice, so you want to demonstrate it as often as possible. Intelligent people earn others' respect.

But intelligence does not result in love.

There are other people who are loved. Only emotion can result in love, for instance, or simplicity, authenticity, demonstrativeness, humour, courtesy, helpfulness and such emotional qualities. In fact you may be less intelligent than another person but may be loved more.

It is possible to track the respect and love inspired by a person or a brand. Box 9.1 illustrates how this was done for Brand Tata.

BOX 9.1

Respecting and loving

During the years that I supervised the Tata brand development, I used to review a half-yearly market feedback data about the perceptions of Brand Tata. Amidst a vast array of data, I would always look for a two-by-two depiction of a key score: Brand Affinity versus Relevance. Put simply, this plotted Affinity on the X axis (how deeply people loved Tata), and Relevance on the Y axis (how strongly they respected Tata).

Brand Tata always appeared at the top right-hand corner, which meant that Brand Tata was uniquely respected in people's minds for its economic performance, and loved in people's hearts for being who Tata is. Other peer corporate brands that the survey tracked were also respected to varying degrees, but not one was loved as deeply Tata was. This was a huge point of brand differentiation. Respondents were emotionally interested and involved with Brand Tata. The data was consistent for all the twenty-two data points between 2001 till 2012 through many highs and controversies.

You could love a person, but how could you love a company? It was a hugely unique position for any company to occupy.

Over the last few years, I have asked many senior corporate leaders about the choice that they would exercise if they had to choose a CEO from between two candidates, both very close in competence and track record. On a nine-point scale of Respect and Love, assume that one scores 8 for 'respected' and 5 for 'loved' while the other candidate is 5 for 'respected' and 8 for 'loved'.

I have been struck by the clarity and consistency of response. Every person I surveyed has chosen the candidate scoring 5 for 'respect', 8 for 'loved'. This has a deep significance. It means that once a person has a qualifying good score (5) level for both personal intelligence and warmth, the warmer person is preferred as a corporate leader as compared to the more intelligent person.

Yet throughout your career, you are focussed on consciously developing your knowledge, communication skills and intelligence and do not pay adequate attention to your human skill development. The preferred profile of the future leader seems to be the opposite!

MR 'WARM' AND MR 'CLEVER'

I have observed a case of leadership choice closely. I should emphasize that both were top-class professionals. I also had the chance to observe the reputations that they left after the choice was made. The case suggests, but does not prove, the point that a warm leader goes a bit longer than a very intelligent leader.

To mask the identity of the persons involved and to make the anecdote meaningful, I use the terms 'warm person' and 'clever person' in the narrative that follows. The terms should be interpreted as a tendency. Both were clever and warm. The only difference was that one was perceived as scoring a sort of 8, 5 and the other, a sort of 5, 8 on the Warmth/Intelligence matrix.

Mr Clever joined as a young trainee after a brilliant academic record: gold medal, first class, distinctions, highly spoken of and all else that goes with highly intelligent people. Once in the company, Clever impressed the seniors and rose rapidly. Challenges were thrown at him and, after the initial adaptation, he met all the challenges successfully. He had a fertile mind with ideas and he always sought ways to tackle the problem by proposing these ideas to his team. He was not a difficult person to get on with but he was not perceived as a warm person. Some subordinates referred to him as a 'cold fish'. He was acknowledged by his peers and subordinates as being very smart and intelligent. In fact his interactions showed him to be smart. In the popular view, Mr Clever was a clear candidate to become the CEO.

Mr Warm was about the same age as Mr Clever. His academic background was very impressive, but not peppered with as many academic accolades and distinctions as his friend's. During his college days, Mr Warm had participated in plays and debates, and interacted with fellow students in extra-mural activities. He too joined the company at a similar time and progressed very fast. He was seen by his superiors as having a way with people. When faced with a challenging situation, he would immediately convene his colleagues and seek their inputs in framing a solution. He had a way with letting his subordinates feel taller when they interacted with him. Some people thought Mr Warm to be less clever than Mr Clever (perhaps because he sought everyone's ideas, whereas Mr Clever would propose solutions himself).

Both got a chance to be the CEO of the same company, one got the opportunity first and the other person a bit later. So now people had views on the relative performance of Mr Clever and Mr Warm in exactly the same job. Both of them had done extremely well. In the intelligence sphere, on the basis of economic performance, both scored highly. But Mr Clever got a bit embroiled in projecting himself in the public domain. Mr Warm always projected his company and not himself. Many people, in a purely anecdotal way, thought that Mr Warm was a 'better leader'. He was more approachable and people felt comfortable with him.

Assuming that there is any materiality to people's views, the perception may well be because of the differences in their human approaches.

SMART SUBORDINATES MAY COME THROUGH AS THREATENING TO THEIR BOSS

In their relentless pursuit of appearing smart, upcoming managers sometimes do not realize that they may appear threatening to their boss. This is not because the boss is a fool; he or she is probably intelligent enough with a score of 5! The perception of being threatening may happen for a number of reasons, which the upcoming manager should be conscious of.

I. *Unknown to you, the boss is going through a lean patch.* Everyone is human, and the boss may be a bit insecure. Your attempt to portray yourself as an intelligent subordinate, especially to his or her boss, may not be interpreted well.

II.*You present yourself to the outside world as stronger than the boss.* You may not be doing so consciously but your behaviour may be having that effect. It is you who needs to be sensitive and consider how to change your behaviour.

III.*You have a solution to every problem, and have time for more.* Some subordinates never seem to be in doubt. If the boss hesitates on a subject because he sees other dimensions, Mr Smart 'cuts through the adipose tissues of the issue' and offers pat solutions.

IV.*You are in reality an uppity little guy with a big head.* Everyone goes through this phase periodically. You have to become more self-aware and pipe down a bit. Remind yourself that the company's really major problems are better solved through human relations rather than through intellect.

I have first-hand experience and observation of being in the kind of situations narrated above—and anyone with forty-five years of management would have the same. Two prominent instructive, documented and public cases, not so widely recalled, are described in Box 9.2.

BOX 9.2

General Sarath Fonseka

Fonseka has been described as Sri Lanka's most successful army commander. As Commander of the Army, Fonseka played an instrumental role in ending the twenty-six-year Sri Lankan Civil War in 2009, defeating the LTTE (Liberation Tigers of Tamil Eelam) in the process. He later had a public falling out with his boss, President Mahinda Rajapaksa. He even challenged Rajapaksa in the 2010 presidential election. Thus Sarath Fonseka is a former commander and general of the Sri Lanka Army and a former candidate for President of Sri Lanka.

Fonseka joined the Sri Lanka Army in 1970 and saw extensive action throughout the long civil war, culminating in a term as Commander of the Army from December 2005 till July 2009. As commander, he oversaw the final phase of the Sri Lankan Civil War, which resulted in the total defeat of the LTTE organization. He also survived an assassination attempt when an LTTE suicide bomber attacked his motorcade in April 2006.

Following the end of the war Fonseka was promoted to a four star rank in the Sri Lanka Army, becoming the first serving officer to hold a four star rank. Fonseka was appointed Chief of Defence Staff by President Mahinda Rajapaksa. While his new post was of a higher rank, Fonseka saw the move as an attempt to sideline him. Amid rumours of his desire to enter politics, he subsequently retired from the post in November 2009 and formally announced his candidature in the 2010 Sri Lankan presidential election.

His candidacy was endorsed by the main opposition parties, and Fonseka became their candidate challenging his old boss, President Rajapaksa. He campaigned under the sign of a swan, and the slogan *Vishvasaniya Venasak* (a credible change).

Unfortunately for him, he lost the election, following which Fonseka was arrested on 8 February 2010, and the government announced he would be court martialled on various charges.

Caroline Kepcher

Kepcher began her foray into business by selling Avon Products door to door. Following high school she took a job as a waitress at a Manhattan restaurant, and ultimately attained the role of manager. She learned teamwork attending Mercy College in nearby Dobbs

Ferry on a volleyball scholarship. She graduated with a marketing degree. Despite having little experience, in 1992 Kepcher secured a position as sales and marketing director of a golf club outside New York City. Her primary responsibility was to prepare the property for bank auction, where it was eventually sold to Donald Trump. Kepcher's ideas on how best to use the property impressed him, and he hired her as director of sales and marketing in 1994.

After four years in this capacity, she was named interim general manager after the existing general manager was ousted from the organization. Her effective management skills convinced Trump of her ability to lead and he later named her the Chief Operating Officer and General Manager of the Trump National Golf Club in Briarcliff Manor, New York, and subsequently the Trump National Golf Club in Bedminster, New Jersey, overseeing over 250 employees at each location.

In 2004, she wrote a business book *Carolyn 101: Business Lessons From the Apprentice's Straight Shooter* based on her business experience. The book went to #2 on the *New York Times* Best Seller List.

On 31 August 2006, Kepcher's employment at the Trump organization ended. According to reports, Trump felt that Kepcher's newfound celebrity status had kept her too busy with speaking engagements and endorsements to focus on her responsibilities to the organization.

Following her departure from the Trump organization, Kepcher became co-founder and CEO of Carolyn & Co., a company created for the purpose of 'providing a broad array of services and assistance to career women'. In 2009, Kepcher was a contributor to Fox Business. Kepcher is still highly regarded in the golf industry, acting as a consultant.

DO NOT ARGUE WITH YOUR BOSS ON BEHALF OF YOUR SUBORDINATES AS A GROUP

A tendency that I have observed in some upcoming executives is picking an argument or fight with the boss on behalf of the subordinates. Howsoever well you present the arguments, you must be aware of the likelihood of coming through as a sort of 'union leader who is trying to make a win to show others'.

First I must specify a caveat. I am not here referring to a case where an issue of ethics or major principle is involved. Neither am I referring to a case where a boss may be prejudiced about one particular officer. Those are cases where you have to state your point of view. The delicate ones I am referring to are situations where you may argue for better terms for 'all marketing people' or for 'my department versus other departments'.

Kumar was a senior HR professional. He had done well in his career and rose to be the head of HR in his company. He had changed a number of jobs during his twenty-five year career. He now joined a larger manufacturing company as the HR head.

In the new company, he found that the leadership was dominated by engineers who had risen from the factories.

They displayed a natural empathy for the role of every senior manager in the factory: the challenges, constraints and the complexities. Kumar found less empathy for the human resources function.

Kumar's sensitivity on this subject was noticed by the other HR managers in the company. They started grumbling to Kumar periodically that they were treated as second-class managers. Their designation and remuneration were evidence of the lower status, according to them. A virtual cycle began whereby Kumar listened to them and they told him more.

It did not take long for Kumar to start raising the issue with his peers and the CEO. Their view was initially sympathetic. They argued that the HR department has to up the game and deliver real value. The HR function, according to them, had become bureaucratic and rule making rather than acting as a partner to the operating managers. Could Kumar work on that before representing the HR folks' grievances?

To Kumar, the matter was confounding. The past behaviour of the leadership had relegated the HR function to a certain pattern. How could he lift the HR contribution until the leadership 'gave HR more respect?' But the leaders wanted the HR game to be upped before they would view HR differently. It was a challenge which Kumar could have handled delicately. But he went at it, hammer and tongs.

No discussion was complete without Kumar making some remark or the other on this subject. His colleagues got fed up of him, as indeed did his CEO. He began to be seen as a sort of union leader, as a manager who was not quite transforming and leading his team. The dynamics deteriorated, initially gradually, and then rapidly. Kumar did not last more than two years!

This kind of dilemma exists in many corporations. It is a challenge for many functional heads and less prominent business heads in a multi-business company. If Kumar had adopted the motto *Deserve before you desire,* would he have thought of a different action plan? Maybe he could have solved the problem!

ADVOCACY

10

COMMUNICATE AND
CARRY CO-WORKERS

Everyone lives by selling something.

—Robert Louis Stevenson

In 1967 I interviewed for a job at Unilever's Indian subsidiary, Hindustan Lever (HLL). I had responded to an advertisement requiring engineers to join the company's prestigious management trainee scheme, but specifically for 'Systems and Procedures'. In those days, it was a zingy terminology; later, the activity came to be called Electronic Data Processing and, finally, Information Technology.

At the final interview at Mumbai, there were three separate events: a group discussion, an interview with a visually-challenged psychologist and a meeting with a heavyweight panel comprising the Personnel Director, Head of Management Services, Head of Selection and the Director of Marketing, an expatriate board member called Scott Birnie.

I wondered what the Marketing Director was doing on the panel. To tell the truth, I was apprehensive that a blue-blooded engineer from an IIT would be seduced to join the Marketing Department, selling Dalda and Sunlight. At that time, I just did not want to do anything in Marketing.

During the interview, the pencil-chewing Birnie asked me an awkward question, 'Gopal, have you ever sold anything?' My response was polite but firm, that I had not tried selling anything, and I was not keen to sell anything. After all, I had studied engineering! To my naïve and young mind, there were two different worlds —people who sold (hucksters) and serious professionals (who used their mind, such as engineers)!

Scott tossed me his pencil and said, 'Why don't you try to sell me this pencil?' I was really shocked. I mumbled something, suppressed my irritation and made a go of the situation. To me the effort was unsatisfactory and weak. To him, it must have seemed better because he said, 'If you are selected, you can work in the Systems Department as you desire, but if you ever get bored and want to be a marketer, just walk into my office.'

I thanked him for the offer, I prayed that the ordeal was over, and swore that I would never walk into Scott Birnie's office to become a marketer.

Later in this chapter, I will tell the story of how I did walk in four years later, not into Scott Birnie's office, but into the office of his successor, David Webb.

For many years I reflected on what Scott Birnie must have been trying to assess. I think he was checking to see whether I had an 'attitude of advocacy'.

Advocacy Is a Hugely Value-adding Skill

To earn a living, every person has to try to advocate an idea to someone or persuade someone to buy something. It may be a porter negotiating to carry the traveller's suitcase, a fruit seller trying to supply his wares to a customer, a college professor imparting education to students, an executive making suggestions to his departmental head, a factory manager explaining a factory requirement to an industrial authority or a chairman presenting an investment case to a minister. Every one of them uses the skill of advocacy. We all have to sell a product, a service or an idea to add value.

That is why the role I respect vastly is that of sales folk. The shop assistant in the departmental store, the itinerant grocery salesman, the soap, car or insurance sales person, all of these people play crucial roles at the precise point where the rubber hits the road.

Put more broadly, the real value addition in all corporate jobs happens when you are able to sell someone else a product, a service or an idea. This requires you to combine the skills of communicating, convincing and carrying people, the totality of which is the skill of advocacy.

Absence of the skill of advocacy is a big block, which limits the effectiveness, and hence the progress, of many executives.

David Novak has written about his conversation with the fabled Jack Welch when Novak had been appointed the first-time CEO of YUMS, the spin-off food company from Pepsi.[1] Novak noted several points of advice from Jack, and asked at the end of his interview, 'If you were in my position, starting a new company, what would you do?' Welch replied, 'Looking back at my career in GE, one of the things I wish I could do over is I wish I would've talked to our people more about what kind of company I envisioned us to be . . . what our values were and what we really stood for.'

ADVOCACY IS FINE, BUT OF WHOSE OPINION?

As you climb the corporate ladder, you are boss to subordinates, you are subordinate to your boss, and you also have a number of peers as colleagues. To advocate solutions to problems or new thoughts, you will advance your own ideas. A terrific augmentation is to assemble the best from all those around who have ideas, obviously taking care not to usurp the credit for others' ideas. Through this practice you can become a great advocate of ideas and solutions in business.

A philosophical point and a mindset issue offer themselves for thought. If you are convinced that you are very smart, you tend not to listen to others carefully or take their views seriously. You then become a regular purveyor of your own ideas.

On the other hand, you may genuinely believe that 'None of us is smarter than all of us put together.' Then you approach human transactions with a sense of humility and you listen to others to seek the best points of each conversation. You really believe that it matters not who thought of the idea, it matters more who did something useful with the idea. You tend to start your conversations with statements like, 'As Mahesh said . . .,' rather than, 'I have always known that . . .'

TATA GROUP INNOVATION FORUM

In an internal conference in 2004, Chairman Ratan Tata exhorted the leadership of Tata companies to figure out how to make their units more innovative. He emphasized the importance of organizational culture, namely, building an innovative culture in all Tata companies, not merely installing innovation processes. Later I accepted an invitation to chair the Tata Group Innovation Forum, TGIF. My implementation colleagues were from a department called Tata Quality Management Services.

I was struck by the way the implementation team of Sunil, Ravi and several others went about their tasks over the next few years. They became willing and enthusiastic recipients of many people's ideas and followed up by becoming advocates for the ideas approved for implementation by the TGIF.

The mandate for the TGIF initially was fuzzy, made more so by the fact that we were to deal with culture. It would have been so much easier to deal with processes. Further the Tata companies work like a federation of units, not through command and control as many other business groups do.

In such a situation, you have to learn new skills. You have to learn the art of getting into the heads of others and understand what makes another person suggest whatever is being suggested. You must really believe that it is easier to make powerful ideas from multiple sources more practical than to make pedestrian ideas become more powerful.

Ravi, Sunil and others behaved like blue jays, which are known to be very collaborative. They would flit from company to company within Tata and outside, document best experiences, talk to academics, cooperate with the Tata Management Training Centre and, in short, do whatever it took to develop an actionable agenda for innovation. I was always struck that more often than not, Ravi would start his presentations by saying, 'As XYZ suggested, we tried this,' or

'This idea has been adapted from what we observed in Israel.' Sunil and Ravi relied on advocacy all the time—to develop an agenda of work for TGIF and, in the process, they honed their personal skills.

OBSTACLES TO ADVOCACY

The obstacle to successful advocacy may lie beyond an individual. The boss may not be receptive to new ideas, the atmosphere may be unprofessional or political, and the company may be putting down uppity youngsters; all of this, and worse, is possible. If you get to work in such a company, clear out fast into a new one. Do not hang in there and complain. You too will become a Luddite in due course.

The company should be expected to be imperfect and have a few glitches. So is every company in the world. You should then look inwards at what could be standing in the way of new ideas being advocated and adopted. It could be you.

- You may think you are smarter than all the others. You may lack the motivation to engage in advocacy.
- You may have lost self-esteem because you tried to advocate a point of view on some earlier occasion but it was not accepted. Advocacy is like sports; you win some and you lose some.
- You are unable to counter an alternative viewpoint because the other person is coming on quite heavily. This is the whole point about advocacy as a skill. The person who comes on hardest is not the one who has the better ideas.
- You are afraid your idea will be hijacked, mutilated or changed. This suggests that you need to re-examine what brainstorming and ideation is all about.

How I Ended Up in Marketing

These days we cannot think of a world without computers and Information Technology. That was not the world when I began to work in 1967. There were only a few mainframe computers in all of India: a couple at some research laboratories, and just a couple imported by private firms, including IBM who needed to showcase their services. In that atmosphere labour unions were opposed to computerization as they felt threatened. Computers—not their operation but the possibility of their introduction—led to strikes and lock-outs. It was a world without even pocket calculators: my engineering slide rule was the prevailing masterpiece of computing!

It was in this atmosphere that HLL decided to introduce computers. There had been some prior experience in the company with tabulators and Hollerith machines. The leadership of the company felt that it was the right time to consider the introduction of computers. Soon after I joined, the company ordered an IBM 1401, then cancelled it, and finally ordered an ICL 1901 machine. One of my roles was to assist and sell the idea of computers to a management that had managed perfectly well without them for decades.

It was one hell of a training ground in advocacy during those early years. I was young, brash and humility was not one of my virtues. What seemed obvious to me just did not appear so to the others. My task was to map out the sales processes, automate them and serve the sales managers with a better information system. I loved the technical aspects of my job: the mapping of the existing processes, the analysis of its strengths and weaknesses, the writing of programs, debugging programs and, in short, doing a whole lot of clever things to solve pretty simple problems! You think I was in a mood to 'sell ideas' to people who did not want those ideas? Not really, but I was forced to learn the skills of advocacy.

Collectively our department could not progress the agenda. Our department could get budget sanctions for more systems analysts and programmers while line departments could not get approval for an extra sales manager or sales planner. A 'revolution' in information flow in the company had been forecast and perhaps recruits like myself were seen as the 'revolutionaries' by a budget-starved set of line managers. As young managers, we criticized the line managers and leadership. We just could not appreciate that it was our job to sell our services.

Business conditions deteriorated for the company. The directors decided that it was too costly to computerize at that stage. The ICL 1901 machine order was cancelled. Our whole department was wound up. That is when I visited David Webb to ask if I could sell Dalda and Sunlight. And, professionally speaking, I had moved on to another domain.

CIRCLES OF ADVOCACY

The demands of advocacy evolve into widening circles as you move in your career path. The case of Arup as narrated in the first chapter illustrates the circles.

Arup first ran a small department within a large factory. Then he got a chance to run his own small factory far away from the head office. Finally he got a chance to run the whole company. As he progressed, the circles of advocacy widened. From persuading people who reported to him, the circle widened to include people who did not report to him. Such a progression happens to every person.

In the innermost circle, you are placed in a role where your resources are specified and it is possible to define your tasks and deliverables clearly. For instance, the task may be to use your team of ten salesmen in Tamil Nadu to distribute and sell the company products widely and efficiently. The measures of efficiency may be specified through sales volume targets, outlet coverage and sales calls per day. You are really being tested to deliver target outputs through clearly allocated resources.

In the second circle, you have a more senior role. You have to work collaboratively with other functional managers. You are not responsible for the logistics, finance or legal functions but you are required to work with those colleagues to achieve goals. You realize the need to learn how to deliver results when all the required resources do not report to you. Here is where your skills of advocacy really start to get tested.

In the third circle, you have overall corporate responsibility for, say, sales and marketing. You have little to do with manufacturing or quality but their work and priorities impact your output.

Learning Advocacy and Persuasion

If you need to develop an argument regarding an issue about which you feel very strongly, sometimes rhetoric is less helpful than storytelling. Do something that effectively delivers a message, says John Baldoni, a leadership author.[2]

'Effective storytelling can serve anyone in leadership who seeks to persuade others to his or her point of view. Opinion-based rhetoric is often more polarizing than persuasive; while statistics are often "go in one ear and out the other". But a careful blending of rhetoric and facts, woven into the right story, can change minds,' says Baldoni.

His suggestions about how to shape a story appear in Box 10.1.

BOX 10.1: STORYTELLING FOR PERSUASION

Know your message. When it comes to persuasion we resist being told what to think but we are open to why we must think it. Good stories have more than a point of view; they have a message. As such they are tools of persuasion. You consider what you want others to do and why you want them to do it. That is your message.

Find the right example. Look for what people around you are doing that relates to your point of view. If you want to persuade people to adopt safety standards, tell the story of what happened when someone did not follow protocol. If you want to demonstrate the benefits of a new process, use a story.

Weave your narrative. It is best to use real-life examples. Therefore, talk about what an employee did to ensure safety or how a team adopted a new process and achieved improved results. Tie to a narrative by following strong story structure. Describe the situation. Talk about what happened. Close with the benefits pitch.

Convey passion. You don't need to go overboard, but you do need to demonstrate your conviction. Do this through your choice of words—ones that draw pictures.

And do it through your delivery—raising your voice on a key point, pausing for emphasis and following through with well-paced flow.

Support with facts. Using a narrative approach doesn't mean you can't use facts. Weave them into your narrative, or begin or end your story with them. For example, one in four children is falling behind in math by the third grade. So if you're trying to convince people this is a problem worth addressing, you might say, 'Let me tell you the story of Daniel, a fourth grader at Summit Elementary . . .' Then you sketch the story. And perhaps after telling Daniel's story, you close with a few more facts about the need for remedial math schooling.

As powerful as storytelling can be, it may not be appropriate for every occasion. Sometimes you need to get to the point. And the best way to relate your point of view, especially with a business case, is to do it quickly and concisely. In these situations, facts and figures are a story in themselves. Stories are powerful when put in the hands of leaders who know how to use them.

—Excerpted with permission from
John Baldoni, a leadership author[2]

Stories Are Not a Management Fad

Think of the best lessons you have learnt about soft subjects like character, self-esteem and honesty.[3] Almost always, the lesson is associated with an anecdote from your own experience or an interaction with somebody you respect or a story told by somebody.

There are traditions of storytelling in India that have evolved over the centuries, for example, the *jatra* in rural Bengal, the *upanyasam* in Tamil Nadu, the *harikathaa* in the north are regional expressions of education and entertainment rolled into one. This is so in other countries too.

The drama of human emotion is a great preservative for ideas, because both the idea and the drama get indelibly etched in your mind—the selflessness of Hanuman, the righteousness of Yudhisthira, Aesop's hare and tortoise, the love of Heer and Ranjha, and so on. The strong connection between learning on the one hand and anecdotes and stories on the other is because an idea is united with an emotion.

That is why stories are a very important way of persuasion, especially on fuzzy and complex subjects. When it comes to ethical and religious studies, and subjects such as good character, good citizenry, and good social values, storytelling is effective.

A big part of an executive's job is to motivate people to reach certain goals. To do that, he or she must engage their emotions, and the key to their hearts is a story. And successful managers know that they cannot thrive by selling pipe dreams or by communicating via spin doctors. They must engage with their managers, look them in the eye and say, 'We'll be lucky as hell if we get through this, but here is what I think we should do.' And they will listen to him.

I have witnessed this during my career, and indeed practised it, especially in situations of turnaround: Etah Dairy, Lever Exports in Hindustan Lever, Unilever Arabia, and some of the Tata companies with which I have been associated. Getting the best out of the people who know the business well is so very important—yet one needs to do so at a time when they are least motivated to open up and share their views.

In the May 2004 issue of *Harvard Business Review*, Stephen Denning wrote an article entitled 'Telling Stories'. In his workplace at the World Bank, his function was knowledge management. Like many managers, he too believed that analytical was good; anecdotal was bad. All of business thinking and training is about being rational, analytical and logical— almost as though, once the logic is clear to someone, he will do the obvious! Yet, every manager knows that is not true.

Analysis may excite the mind, but it rarely offers a route to the heart. Not surprisingly, Stephen Denning found it an uphill task to persuade his World Bank colleagues to accept knowledge management through his logical PowerPoint presentations. He then told them a 150-word story about a health worker in Zambia. It brought out a human perspective, packed with emotion, about the state of the problem as perceived by the grassroots-level worker. He was amazed that his audience at the World Bank was now 'connecting'!

Hollywood's top screen-writing coach, Robert Mckee, is a PhD in cinema arts. His students have written, directed and produced winning films like *Forrest Gump*, *Erin Brockovich*, *Gandhi* and many others. Mckee feels that executives can engage listeners on a whole new level if they toss out their PowerPoint slides and learn to tell good stories instead, because 'stories fulfil a profound human need to grasp the patterns of living— not merely as an intellectual exercise, but within a very personal, emotional experience'. In a story, you not only weave a lot of information into the telling but you also arouse your listener's emotions and energy. Storytelling is related to management.

11

INTERACT WITH AND CARRY ALL STAKEHOLDERS

In a free enterprise, the community is not just another stakeholder in business, but is in fact the very purpose of its existence.

—Jamsetji N. Tata

The wealth gathered by Jamsetji Tata and his sons in half a century of industrial pioneering formed but a minute fraction of the amount by which they enriched the nation. The whole of that wealth is held in trust for the people and used exclusively for their benefit. The cycle is thus complete. What came from the people has gone back to the people many times over.

—J.R.D. Tata

Is a manager's responsibility solely to manage the business or something more? If it is more, who is to determine what

156

else? And once what else is clear, who is to determine how much? This subject has waxed and waned during the twentieth century.

Management has evolved as a profession principally in free-enterprise America, promoted by the early establishment of academic business schools. That is why management theories and pedagogy have emanated prolifically from America.

During the first half of the twentieth century, American business grew to be very big and started to get involved in all sorts of activities, both business and non-business. Conglomerates were pervasive and powerful in America. Periodically there would be a debate on how to limit large companies and how much they should be involved in non-business activities, including society and politics.

As I began my career during the last half century, managers were often portrayed as though they had virtually an unfettered right to run and grow their business so long as they diligently paid their taxes, benevolently looked after their employees, and remunerated their shareholders.

However, an alternative viewpoint started to emerge from sections of society who had a different take on the subject. Initially these unorganized sections were seen as a nuisance or as cranks until they developed into a force that could threaten or thwart companies. During the 1980s the labour unions were considered obstructionist and untrustworthy during the Thatcher-Reagan period. Large companies were initially thought to do no harm to natural resources until environmentalist Rachel Carson led her movement against the spraying of DDT. She argued that uncontrolled use of DDT and pesticides caused immense damage to the environment. Her book *Silent Spring* could be considered as the beginning of the movement which today we refer to as the sustainability movement.

Large companies were found to gang up and charge unwary consumers cartel prices, thus enriching themselves. Anti-monopolistic legislation was imposed and a permanent cat-and-mouse game would be enacted between large companies and regulators from time to time. Some big companies indulged in activities which would be unthinkable today; they were seen as rogues, capitalist ogres operating around the world, controlling and terrorizing poor countries. One early example that I recall was the ITT's involvement in politics. See Box II.I.

BOX 11.1

ITT Company activities

The International Telephone & Telegraph, ITT, was formed in 1920, created by two broker brothers. Over the next three decades, the brothers acquired several companies in the telephony business and built up their empire across countries including the United States.

Nazi involvement

According to Anthony Sampson's book *The Sovereign State of ITT*, one of the first US businessmen Hitler received after taking power in 1933 was Sosthenes Behn, then the CEO of ITT. Antony C. Sutton, in his book *Wall Street and the Rise of Hitler*, makes the claim that ITT subsidiaries made cash payments to the SS leader, Heinrich Himmler.

In the 1960s, ITT Corporation won $27 million in compensation for damage inflicted on its plant by Allied bombing during World War II. In addition, Sutton's book uncovers that an ITT company made radio and radar parts that were used in the war.

In 1959, Harold Geneen became CEO. Using leveraged buyouts, he turned the business into a major force during the 1960s. ITT's sales grew from about $700 million in 1960 to about $8 billion in 1970, and its profit from $29 million to $550 million.

Involvement in the 1964 coup in Brazil

João Goulart was the president of Brazil. The US government felt that he had Communist leanings. ITT owned the phone company of Brazil; Washington was afraid he would nationalize it. ITT's president, Harold Geneen, was friends with the CIA Director John McCone. The CIA worked against Goulart, performed character assassination, pumped money into opposition groups, and engineered the 1964 Brazilian coup d'état. McCone went to work for ITT a few years later.

Involvement in 1973 Pinochet coup in Chile

In 1970, ITT owned 70 per cent of Chitelco, the Chilean telephone company. Declassified documents released by the CIA in 2000 suggest that ITT financially helped opponents of Salvador Allende's government prepare a military coup. On 28 September 1973, an ITT building in New York City was bombed for alleged involvement in the overthrow of the democratically elected socialist government in Chile.

Activities in Nigeria

The song 'International Thief Thief' by Fela Kuti documents the alleged corruption and meddling of the company in Nigerian politics.

On September 13, 1970, in a *New York Times* magazine article, the economist Milton Friedman argued that the sole purpose of businesses is to generate profit for shareholders. Moreover, he maintained, companies that did adopt 'responsible' attitudes would be faced with more binding constraints than companies that did not, rendering them less competitive. 'What does it mean to say that the corporate executive has a "social responsibility" in his capacity as businessman?' asked Friedman in his article.

Two years later, in 1972, the sales of a management book for the first time crossed the sales of Alex Comfort's book on *The Joy of Sex* in the *New York Times* list of bestsellers in the non-fiction category. The management book was by Peter Drucker.

There were two consequences: first, the profile of management as a profession was dramatically increased and second, the single-mindedness of profit as the sole purpose of a business took deep root.

LEGITIMACY FOR MANAGERS' INVOLVEMENT WITH STAKEHOLDERS

It was not until 1984 that an argument was put forward in favour of stakeholders rather than shareholders exclusively. The stakeholder theory is a theory of organizational management and business ethics that addresses morals and values in managing an organization. It was originally detailed by R. Edward Freeman in the book *Strategic Management: A Stakeholder Approach*, which identified the groups who were stakeholders of a corporation. The book described and recommended methods by which management can give due regard to the interests of those groups. In short, it attempted to address the 'Principle of Who or What Really Counts.'

Stakeholders are the aggregation of all constituencies with a stake in the business, apart from the owners: employees, vendors and partners, government, community and society.

Viewing the subject from an Indian perspective, the late development of the stakeholder and related concepts in the west appears strange. As early as the 1880s, Jamsetji Tata, the founder of the Tata companies, had stated exactly the opposite of Milton Friedman as demonstrated by the quotation at the head of this chapter. Sixty years later, in different words, Jamsetji's idea was repeated by his successor, J.R.D. Tata, as the second quotation shows.

The stakeholder has always been at the centre of the way Tata companies ran the business.

Management teaching and practice in the first ten years of an upcoming executive's career is focussed on mastering techniques to maximize efficiency and profits from given resources. The interaction and interdependence between a company and its stakeholders does not occupy much of the attention of the upcoming manager. That engagement comes only later.

When managers enter a company, they are trained to deal with the levers of the business; they grow up somewhat insulated from many of these other stakeholders. It is only around mid-career that they begin to interact with some of them.

Recall how Arup (Chapter 1) had to deal with the government officials, the employee union, local politicians and so many others. To be successful in his job, he just had to interact with these people and find a way to carry them with him. These interactions were a source of new learning for him.

STAKEHOLDER MANAGEMENT WILL BE A KEY SKILL FOR THE FUTURE

Government, civil society and media are some key members of the stakeholder community.

There are many forms of governance in the world. After the fall of communism, a widely held view was that all nations and societies will converge to the so-called western model. In the film, *The Iron Lady,* a memorable scene is when the prime minister, Margaret Thatcher, tells a protesting Geoffrey Howe, who was her longest serving cabinet minister, 'Geoffrey, we have been elected to act and to solve real problems, not to keep winning elections.' There is no Iron Lady left.

In 1989, economist John Williamson had described a set of policies for economic reform called the Washington Consensus. His model had six principles: quality governing institutions, free markets, rule of law, liberal democracy, open markets, and good corporate governance. Unfortunately, even the west has fallen shy of these standards. Democracy everywhere tempts politicians to make unaffordable promises and also dissuades politicians from attempting difficult reforms.

East Asian leaders like Lee Kuan Yew and Mahathir Mohammed have long advocated the Asian Way. China has shown exceptional and dramatic growth through its model of authoritarian capitalism, a term coined by Stefan Halper in *The Beijing Consensus*.

Convergence to the western model has not happened, and will not happen. New forms of governance have emerged. Therefore, future managers just have to master the skills of dealing with the government and its constituencies in developed as well as emerging markets.

Civil society is far better organized nowadays. Corporations may feel hassled when they have to deal with the objections of civil society; however, mature and upcoming company officers realize that, by and large, NGOs and conscientious objectors also have a positive role to play in the evolution of society. There is a Rachel Carson for every subject from sustainability and inclusive growth to globalization and extraction of natural resources.

Therefore, it is crucial for the upcoming executive to learn the advocacy skills required to deal effectively with such institutions.

Finally, it is appropriate to say a word about the media. When I began my career in socialist India, the media avoided business and conversely. Now we have in India a vibrant scene in which every publication and channel is 'breaking news' even when the news is already 'broken'.

All said and done, they are one of the four estates of a

democracy. Company managements have learnt to deal with the other estates of a democracy, but many find the media difficult to deal with. This only highlights and confirms the need for the upcoming executive to learn the advocacy skills required to interact with and carry all stakeholders.

GAINING EXPERIENCE IN DEALING WITH STAKEHOLDERS

Upcoming executives should welcome a development stint in functions such as Government Relations, Media Communications and Public Affairs. These are not castaway roles or ones to be shunned.

In hindsight I was given exposure when I was a young officer of ten years' experience at HLL. Chairman Thomas accompanied me on a market tour of Punjab when I was Regional Sales Manager based in Delhi. When we boarded the night train at Amritsar to return to Delhi, he asked me directly, 'How would you like to move to Mumbai to be the company's Corporate Communications manager?' I nearly fell off the train seat and stuttered, 'You must be joking.' He said tersely, 'The chairman of HLL does not joke at 9.30 p.m. with regional managers.'

That is how I returned to Mumbai and learnt how to deal with the media, which, of course, was very different from what it is today. However, I must confess that I met a very different bunch of professionals. I learnt to think about their very different ideas and I learnt to appreciate early on the important societal role that they were playing. During my tenure I assisted the leadership to migrate the HLL logo and positioning from the palm tree and 'Hindustan Lever serves the home' to the green leaf and 'Serving the Nation.' It was an invaluable experience.

Soon after, I was assigned to the Delhi office to hold fort for three months while the regular incumbent, Suman Sinha, went abroad to attend a training course. The company's FERA case was in the crucible at that time. I was incredibly fortunate to watch the strategy being developed and executed by the company chairman himself, to read the advocacy papers, and, in a small way, to participate in the communication exercises while I was in Delhi.

When I joined Tata, of course, I saw corporate sustainability and stakeholder management being practised at a fundamental level and as the very basis of running the business: pretty much as the founder had visualized one hundred years earlier. It seemed effortless because the executives, not just the top leaders, were wired into a way of thinking from their first day.

The responses across diverse Tata companies to stakeholder challenges have been written about in case studies and reports. What is remarkable is that all of the stories and case studies conform to a unified philosophy of stakeholder management— this is almost impossible to design and implement across multiple companies at different points of time.

I reflect on the public affairs and stakeholder responses of Tata companies to diverse issues that have arisen in the course of running the companies: the response to being denied a licence for setting up both airlines and airports, the Tata Tea response to the ULFA issue in Assam, the response to the Tata Finance fraud, the Tata Steel response to the baseless land controversies raised in Orissa and Chattisgarh, the superb execution by Tata Power of the Maithon Power Project, the Tata Motors reaction to the Singur land issue and the Tata

Chemicals response to a premature controversy about mining soda ash in Tanzania. All of these, to my mind, demonstrate a sensitivity to handling and communicating on the issues, even if there were disagreements with the response itself.

The staff response of the Taj Mahal Hotel to the terrorist attack of 26/11 was magnificent and will forever hold a special place in my emotions. Nobody can be trained for such a contingency, but minds can be prepared to prioritize actions. Who did you as an employee owe your responsibility to? How did so many employees figure out what to do? A newspaper report about the HR policies that prepare people appears in Box 11.2.

BOX 11.2: HOW TAJ HOTEL'S HR FOUND 26/11 HEROES

Shrenik Avlani, *Hindustan Times*, Mumbai ,
28 November 2011

The Taj Group of hotels' recruitment system, longer training, emphasis on customer-centric behaviour and respect for elders while hiring and encouraging its staff to improvise rather than do things by the book are the main reasons why the workers of the Taj Mahal Palace Hotel in Mumbai acted the way they did and saved the lives of about 1,500 guests who were in the hotel on 26/11 when terrorists attacked the hotel. This is the case made out by Prof. Rohit Deshpande and Anjali Raina in an article titled 'The Ordinary Heroes of the Taj' which will appear in the December issue of the prestigious journal, *Harvard Business Review*.

The article, a study of the organizational culture and leadership in the Taj Group, recounts how the hotel staff took charge in the crisis situation and led from the front to ensure the safety of guests, first, and colleagues. The Taj employees helped 1,200-1,500 guests escape on a night when 31 people, including 11 hotel employees, died and 28 were injured.

Deshpande is a Sebastian S. Kresge professor of marketing at Harvard and Raina is the executive director of the Harvard Business School India Research Centre in Mumbai.

Deshpande and Raina attribute the response of the Taj employees to the hotel chain's organizational culture in which employees are willing to do almost anything for the guests. The authors contend that the unusual hiring, training and incentive systems of the Taj Group have combined to instill an extremely customer-centric work ethic in the hotel's staff.

Taj prefers to hire from smaller cities rather than metros—Pune, not Mumbai—because that's where traditional Indian values—such as respect for elders and teachers, humility, consideration of others—still hold sway. It hires young people, often straight out of high school, who display three traits: respect for elders, cheerfulness and neediness. The chosen candidates are trained at one of the six residential Taj Group skill-certification centres for 18 months, instead of the industry standard of 12 months.

At the managerial level too, the company recruits from the lower-tier B-schools as they find that MBA graduates from these institutes want to build careers with a single company and tend to fit in better with a customer-centric culture. However, no one was trained for a situation like the one on 26/11.

Despite that the Taj staff displayed leadership skills and formed human chains around guests to ensure their safety. Because all Taj employees are empowered to take decisions as agents of the customer, it makes them feel in command. That night they took the decision and saved their guests first.

Deshpande thought of investigating the link between the Taj Group's HR practice and organizational culture and the way Taj employees acted on 26/11 while working on a case on the brand architecture of Taj Hotels in early 2009.

'After finishing the brand architecture case, I requested and received permission from Mr Ratan Tata to develop a separate case focussing on crisis management and brand recovery. This time it was a video case and was taught starting last year at Harvard Business School,' said Deshpande.

Since the video case did not have enough exposure to the latter topic, Deshpande and Raina decided to delve deeper into the Taj HR processes. Hence the current article in *Harvard Business Review*, said Deshpande.

The interviewees included frontline personnel who had lost friends, colleagues, and family during that terrible crisis—Taj manager Karambir Kang being just one amazingly inspirational example.

An American CEO's View

Charles Koch is the CEO of the world's largest private company and has written a book about his company, KII, standing for Koch Industries Inc.[1]

With respect to stakeholder management (he refers to it as Public Sector Capability), I quote excerpts from his book with his permission:

> KII's lawsuits spilled into the public arena, thus amplifying the negative effect of increased regulation, politicization and litigation ... we decided we must build a world-class public sector capability, which we did, under the leadership of Rich Fink. This was done by applying the five dimensions of Market Based Management (MBM) in legal, government and community relations, communications and compliance ... As a corporation, we not only had to be committed to conducting 'all affairs lawfully and with integrity', we had to develop systems to ensure that every employee was committed to—and able to fully comply with—this primary Guiding Principle.

AUTHENTICITY

12

THE DILEMMAS OF AUTHENTICITY

Authenticity is largely defined by what other people see in you.

—Rob Goffee and Gareth Jones

Whether you are a subordinate or a boss, a husband or a wife, a landlord or a tenant, whoever you may be, you would consider it a virtue to be perceived as authentic. The dictionary definition of authentic is 'conforming to fact and therefore worthy of trust, reliance or belief'. Its synonyms are listed as bona fide, genuine, real, and undoubted.

There really is not much difference between the dictionary definition and the popular understanding. Everybody, just about anybody you can think of, thinks of the word authenticity in a similar way. But if this is the meaning, is it a virtue to be authentic when applied to human relations?

Perhaps not. Life would be impossible if every person said

or did what is really on his or her mind. For example you would make an awful spouse if you were to share every thought or opinion exactly as you think or feel. It would be the same between a boss and a subordinate. In no human relationship can you communicate exactly what you feel.

So does that make you unauthentic? You would not agree with such an assessment!

We associate authenticity with sincerity, honesty and integrity. We assume that it is an innate quality in every human being: that each individual is authentic or is not authentic. We assume that an authentic person is consistently so and conversely, unauthentic people are always so. Authenticity is thought of as the opposite of artifice.

This way of thinking about authenticity is flawed. The reality is that your behaviour is a planned balance between expressing your personality and managing the impressions of those whom you wish to relate with. Yes, managing others, but that does not connote manipulativeness or untruthfulness. The yawning gap between the general imagery and the practice of authenticity causes dilemmas about behavioural ethics.

If you have had a bad experience with a person, you think of that person as unreliable and unauthentic. If someone else has had a good experience with the same person, he or she thinks the opposite. The person is the same but the circumstance of the relationship determines whether or not the person is regarded as authentic or not.

A person who is perceived in the workplace as an authentic manager may be one who is cheating on his wife. An authentic and dutiful son may behave deceitfully to achieve a particular goal. The great Sri Rama in the epic *Ramayana* is held as the epitome of human character and authenticity but the epic contains stories that suggest his judgement was sometimes fallible. These episodes have kept scholars engaged in debate and interpretation for centuries.

AUTHENTICITY IS A HUMAN ISSUE AND A DYNAMIC ONE AS WELL

Authenticity is thought of in management circles as applicable more to leaders. It is true that lack of authenticity hurts more at leadership levels, as is true with many vices and virtues, but it is important to recognize that the subject is really a human issue. You cannot be a good subordinate without the required level of authenticity.

A widely referenced paper on the subject as applied to management appeared in the *Harvard Business Review* a few years ago.[1] The authors argued that if you do not manage your authenticity as a young manager, you will get into trouble very quickly in a leadership role.

I recall Joy, a contemporary of mine from my early days as a young HLL manager. Joy was refreshingly honest in his interactions, he was a great colleague, and was appreciated by all for calling a spade a spade. He was noticed soon because he eschewed the sophisticated turns-of-phrase that the office was used to. For example, on one occasion when an aggressive chairman berated young marketers for not adding enough value, Joy bluntly posed, 'Sir, if you don't want us, just say so and fire all of us!' The chairman backed down a bit.

Additionally Joy was bright and competent, so he rose very fast. When he became senior manager, Joy continued behaving and speaking in the way he always had and was known for. However in his new status, the behavioural expectation was different and Joy was now perceived as being brash, a bit loose-tongued and indiscreet. Needless to add, Joy was nonplussed. He thought he was just being himself.

This anecdote illustrates both the aspects mentioned at the head of this paragraph: that authenticity is a human issue and also that since it keeps changing, it is a dynamic issue.

Authenticity carries two challenges. The first challenge is that your words and actions must match or else nobody will consider you authentic. Secondly, to be considered authentic, you must establish a relationship with another person. Here is an example of what I mean.

I once worked for a senior who would constantly point out to me that he was 'arguing and fighting' for me, my promotion, and my posting. I was intrigued because I was under no particular pressure or vulnerability; so why would he want to show me that he was my goodwill ambassador? Gradually I realized that he wanted to secure my loyalty and enhance our relationship by positioning 'the system' as being unfair or opaque and posing himself as my protector. Through a number of episodes concerning me and colleagues (we youngsters used to exchange notes), we all realized that this senior was not being authentic—at least in this particular respect.

WHAT THEN IS AUTHENTICITY AND WHO IS AUTHENTIC?

Through my experiences, I have concluded that certain aspects of authenticity are really worthwhile to remember.

1. *You have to learn how to manage your authenticity.* Authentic people must have the chameleon's ability to adapt to different

situations. Authenticity is not the same as manipulation. You must learn which personality traits you have to reveal and to whom, depending on what is appropriate. I knew a senior leader who had become a bit stern and distant as he rose vertically in the organization. On his appointment at the pinnacle as managing director, his earliest buddies and colleagues hosted a private dinner party for him where I was also invited. The MD was a different man, laughing, cracking jokes and just having a good time being himself. I admired the manner in which he managed his authenticity.

2. *Authenticity means learning from the muddle of real life.* We have created a utopian imagery in which we dream that we should have fewer and fewer problems as we rise. We yearn for increasing certainty. The reality of life and career is exactly the opposite. You are paid your salary to swim with alligators in a swirling river and still come out winning. You have to be immersed in your work and continuously learn from the muddles of uncertainty, ambiguity and real-life problems. These are the experiences that make a person authentic.

3. *Authenticity comes from common sense and self-awareness.* Authentic people become authentic through experiences and not necessarily through deep meditational techniques or psycho-babble. Authentic people are comfortable with themselves and where they have come from. Personally I am a bit wary of 'Authenticity Consultants'. Yes, they exist, just Google the words! To me, authenticity consulting smacks of a lack of authenticity. To my simple way of thinking, the apostles of authenticity are not too far away from the masters of intrigue.

4. *Authenticity is connected with deep personal and professional relationships.* You can tell an authentic person when you interact with one.

You can equally spot an unauthentic person when you see one. The vast majority of people you will meet will be neither very authentic nor very unauthentic. In fact you will regard as authentic those people with whom you have a great relationship. You judge the authenticity through your relationship.

5. *Authentic people do what they have to because that is what they simply have to do.* Given a difficult circumstance, people will act in a way which truly represents who they are. They are not influenced by the after-effects of their actions or their image of authenticity. When I was a departmental head, I discovered a fraud in my department. After some confusion in my mind, I went straight up to my CEO and told him that I was in trouble. The whole company rallied to rescue me from my predicament. On another occasion when I ran the animal feeds division, there were some bird deaths due to the feed consumed by the birds. I was incensed with my plant incharge who confirmed to the regulator that one of the grinders in the plant was malfunctioning and that the bird deaths may have occurred consequent to consuming the company's feed. I insisted on sacking that plant incharge. In his mind he was being authentic. In my mind I will never know whether I did the right thing or not by asking for his resignation.

DOING WHAT YOU HAVE TO DO

It is inspirational to learn of stories from the world of business and from outside with respect to authenticity. My favourite ones appear below.

GERARD ARPEY

I was impressed with the story concerning American Airlines and its CEO, Gerard J. Arpey, which was much in the news in 2011.

In the US, it is possible for a company to declare bankruptcy under Chapter 11. Among the many provisions of bankruptcy laws, several people-related issues get adversely affected: the employees' pensions, termination of retiree medical benefits, changes of labour contracts and work rules. Most CEOs would see these as necessary evils to rescue the company.

Gerard Arpey had served American Airlines for thirty years before becoming the CEO. He had for long held the view that bankruptcy was an improper act, bordering on being immoral, as the *New York Times* report highlighted.[2] Common employees and retirees get affected badly while the CEO walks off with a handsome severance package as per his or her contract. Within his own airline industry, Arpey noted that many companies had filed for bankruptcy. In each of these cases, the bankruptcy gave the airlines the chance to cancel their debt, get rid of the responsibility for employee pensions and renegotiate favourable terms with labour unions.

'I believe it's important to the character of the company and its ultimate long-term success to do your very best to honour those commitments. It is not good thinking to believe you can simply walk away from your circumstances,' he argued. He did all he could until 2010 to save his airline. The board decided it had to act. The company filed for bankruptcy.

Arpey stepped away with no severance package and nearly worthless stock holdings. He just could not get himself to lead an organization which had chosen what he thought was an immoral path.

CAPTAIN HENRIK KURT CARLSEN

One of the biggest stories of 1951 broke just after Christmas when thirty-seven-year-old Capt. Carlsen's ship *Flying Enterprise* was caught in the worst Atlantic storm in fifty years just off the coast of England. For two weeks the world followed the story as it unfolded.

The captain had ordered his forty-member crew and ten passengers off the ship. Carlsen felt that he had to remain on board as long as she remained afloat. If he left the ship, anyone could put a man on the ship and claim it. 'It was my duty to take my ship around the world. It would have been morally wrong to leave,' he later said. The sixty-foot waves battered the ship over the next fifteen days. Finally, after all attempts to rescue the vessel failed, the captain jumped from the listing ship and swam to safety.

He was surprised to find cheering crowds waiting for him at the port in Falmouth. He was cheered as a hero then and on many subsequent occasions. He just could not appreciate why. After all he had merely done his duty.

He was offered large sums by newspapers for an exclusive story and approached by Hollywood with a big offer too. However, he turned them all down. 'I do not want a seaman's honest attempt to save his ship used for any commercial purpose,' he said. The only offer he accepted was the chance to captain *Flying Enterprise II.* He is the subject of a book by Frank Delaney, *Simple Courage: A True Story of Peril on the Sea.*

In an interview many decades later, a journalist asked him what lesson he had learned. 'To do what you are supposed to do,' was his reply.

I have observed that authentic people are quick to admit

when they have bungled or botched up. It may be at work or it may be in a personal relationship. They confront the reality, accept their mistake and get right out to do what is necessary. Authentic people are deeply comfortable with themselves and where they have come from. They always remember who they are—which is the title of the next chapter.

13

REMEMBER WHO YOU ARE

Be yourself; everyone else is already taken.

—Oscar Wilde

The Phoebus Apollo temple at Delphi has two phrases carved into the stone 'Know Thyself' and 'Nothing in Excess'. These two statements (and many other features) have made the Oracle of Delphi famous universally. Over the centuries, there have been many interpretations of those words as well as debates by philosophers and scholars.

If the Oracle tells you to know yourself, imagine how much more difficult it is when someone advises you to just 'Be yourself'. How can you be what you do not know?

In the previous chapter I had observed that authentic people always remember who they are and where they came from and what shaped them to be who they are. Such authentic people act in line with their inner self, irrespective of the consequences.

CONSEQUENCES ARE IRRELEVANT WHEN YOU ACT AS WHO YOU ARE

I feel inspired to recall two stories. The consequences were of no importance to their protagonists. One story is of the well-known, five-hundred-year-old incident of Thomas More in the times of King Henry VIII. The second is a relatively unknown but contemporary story of Bob Kearns, a genius who invented the intermittent wiper.

SIR THOMAS MORE: THE KING'S GOOD SERVANT, BUT GOD'S FIRST

Very briefly, Thomas More was an influential and principled person, who behaved in line with what he believed, even though his stand went against the demands of the reigning emperor King Henry VIII. Thomas More was incarcerated in the Tower of London and was executed. His principles were interred with his bones.

Thomas More was born in 1478 to a prominent judge. He studied at fine institutions and served in the household of an archbishop, who predicted that young Thomas would become a 'marvellous man'. More went on to study classics and law at the most prestigious colleges then available. However, More did not follow his father's profession of law though he had qualified in the subject.

Perhaps his association with the archbishop influenced him but he felt a serious calling to the monastic service. While at Lincoln's Inn, he determined to become a monk and subjected himself to the discipline of a nearby monastery, taking part in the monastic life. The habits of prayer, fasting, and penance stayed with him for the rest of his life. More's desire for monasticism was finally overcome by his sense of duty to serve his country. He entered Parliament in 1504.

During the next two decades, More attracted the attention of King Henry VIII in several ways. He was given challenging public assignments, all of which he discharged with great distinction. More had garnered Henry's favour, and was made Speaker of the House of Commons in 1523 and Chancellor of the Duchy of Lancaster in 1525. In his capacity as Speaker, he helped to establish the parliamentary privilege of free speech.

The conflicts between who he was and his duties seem to have emerged in the public domain when the king wanted to divorce and re-marry, a practice that the Catholic Church did not approve of. The religious orientation of More and its influence must have played a strong role in his refusing to endorse King Henry VIII's plan to divorce Catherine of Aragon in 1527.

Thomas More's fall came quickly and was probably due to his disapproval of Henry's stance toward the church. He refused to attend the coronation of Anne Boleyn in 1533. He also refused to swear to the Act of Succession and the Oath of Supremacy, and was committed to the Tower of London. More was found guilty of treason and was beheaded. His final words on the scaffold were: 'The King's good servant, but God's first.'

Robert Kearns: Accomplished but Frustrated Inventor

When Bob Kearns died of cancer at the age of 77 in February 2005, the *Washington Post* described him as an accomplished but frustrated inventor. 'Robert Kearns's battles with the world's automotive giants have come to an end. Kearns devoted decades of his life to fighting Ford Motor Co., Chrysler Corp. and other carmakers in court, trying to gain the credit he thought he deserved as the inventor of the intermittent windshield wiper,' the *Post* reported. Kearns carried his lonely fight all the way to the Supreme Court, a crusader for the rights of the individual, as many saw him.

When he died at 77, of brain cancer complicated by Alzheimer's disease, Kearns had gained some vindication in the form of $30 million in settlements from Ford and Chrysler, but he never got what he had always sought.

All he wanted, he often said, was the chance to run a factory with his six children and build his wiper motors, along with a later invention for a windshield wiper that was activated automatically by rainfall. In the end, his courtroom battles cost him his job, his marriage and, at times, his mental health.

The story went, doubted by some, that he got his idea on his wedding night in 1953, when a champagne cork struck him in the left eye. The eye eventually became blind. The blinking of his eye led him to wonder if he could make windshield wipers that would move at intervals instead of in a constant back-and-forth motion.

After years of experiments, Kearns believed his invention was ready. He applied for patents, mounted his wipers on his car and drove to Ford's headquarters. At one point, engineers there wondered if he was activating the wipers with a button in his pocket.

It was very difficult to live with someone so obsessed. His wife had had enough. When their divorce was granted in 1989, Kearns was in the midst of his court case against Ford. Although his wife remarried, she continued to support her ex-husband.

In the end having dismissed his lawyers, an exhausted Kearns was unable to manage his multiple lawsuits on his own. When he missed deadlines for filing papers in his cases against General Motors and German and Japanese auto companies, the District Judge, Avern Cohn, dismissed the remaining cases.

By then, Kearns's patents had expired, having passed the seventeen-year window of ownership then in effect. He bought a house and went into retirement. From time to time, he would call his children and his lawyer and talk about reclaiming his patents. As friends would recall though, he was a man of many talents, and it was a rich and colourful life before the patents became an obsession.

Why I Am Who I Am

These examples speak for themselves as to why those people did what they did: they were acting with authenticity and they were acting out of their innermost beliefs, which were born out of their experiences. The same thing happens to all of us. Every person, famous or not-so-famous, has his own life experiences and life lessons, which define who he or she is. Family and childhood background matter, but personal experiences matter much more. Otherwise siblings would be similar. But they are not.

As an example, I draw attention to a number of life stories of accomplished but ordinary people all of which have been put together in an eminently readable book.[1] It is very educative to contemplate your own life story, and better still, write it up. Your self-exercise will be of great value to yourself. You have yours as a distinctive story as indeed I have mine.

I wrote mine as a summary and I narrate it here merely to

illustrate how I remind myself of who I am. It may not be generally inspiring to recall who I am, but I do feel more aware of myself in the same way that the Oracle of Delphi had advised.

Both my parents were born in small villages in Tamil Nadu— Vilakudi and the other Gobi; they were 400 km apart. Neither of my parents could secure an education beyond school. My father devised an ingenious plan to leave the stultifying atmosphere of his village and join his elder brother in the city in order to seek a life of opportunity—in Kolkata, which was quite a vibrant metropolis during the 1930s.

In due course, through determination and positivity, he worked up his way to acquire a professional accountancy qualification and rose impressively to become a senior departmental manager in a multinational company. My mother supported my father as a housewife in the task of raising a large family.

As future events would show, both of them were quick learners and highly adaptive; they were savvy and smart. They adapted to the city ways and learnt how to advance their economic and family life. But at heart, they were both village folk with simple values. At home we used to eat a traditional meal in a traditional way, after saying a prayer of thanks for the meal to follow. My father would shop astutely at the vegetable market every week to stock up (there was no refrigerator at home) and to keep in touch with the reality of household costs. My mother cooked initially, and even in later years, she was closely involved with what was served on the table.

Both of them would narrate to us the stories of village life and about our grandparents. Our parents ensured that the story of the great epics reached our ears, and that the lilts of the Carnatic music lessons for my sisters positively influenced our sensibilities—as much as we used to read Shakespeare and the Bible at school.

My parents hugely emphasized education probably because neither of them could acquire a basic college degree. 'I want all my children to get a degree, and possibly a double degree,' my mother would emphasize, often dreamily; the message was dinned into our tiny heads.

To her credit, each one of us did accomplish her desire. Her passion that her children should study was briefly threatened when my father had no regular job for four years. During that period, my parents stubbornly cut all expenses other than education, enabling my brother to go to England for study, my sister to stand first in her university degree, and the rest of us younger kids to suffer no dilution in the education received. Bless my mother's soul, her grandchildren have done even better.

Father was generous in some ways (like helping indigent relatives financially), but was also very careful with expenditure in other ways (like taking exciting holiday breaks or dining out). He would despise any form of borrowing. Though he had never studied Shakespeare, he would lyrically quote, 'Neither a borrower nor a lender be' as often as he could. 'Spend only from what you earn' and 'Deserve before you desire' were two mottos he dinned into us.

In my professional career, I am considered to be generally averse to borrowing, and certainly opposed to excessive borrowing. Some of my colleagues think that I am conservative in financial terms. May be I am. Perhaps the attitude was fixed in me by what I experienced early at home.

Another influence on my young mind began when I joined college. When I started to stay at the college hostel, the Jesuitin-charge offered me the opportunity to teach evening classes to the underprivileged children of the locality. 'You are so fortunate to get the education you have got, can you spare some time to teach less lucky kids?' he asked. How could one refuse? I think I taught well. I certainly I got a great joy out of teaching; I used to think I was spreading hope. Over time I so dearly wanted others to have some of the privilege of the learning I had received. I learnt what it is to care and share through teaching.

At the college-leaving stage I seriously considered becoming a researcher and a teacher. The poor remuneration discouraged me. Finally I found a way to earn through a business career but get the satisfaction of teaching through my spare-time activities.

I have continued some form of teaching right through my career. My HLL export department colleagues and I taught a foreign trade course at Bombay University in the 1980s when foreign trade was a non-event in India. Many years after my graduation, my teacher, the late Prof G.S. Sanyal, requested me to teach at the Vinod Gupta School of Management on the IIT campus, I took leave from work and camped at IIT to fulfil my promise to him. Even these days I teach a credit course at B-schools entitled LWNT, standing for 'Learning What's Not Taught.'

It is perhaps the same satisfaction of sharing that has given me the motivation and energy to write this book, and the two earlier ones. I know that 90 per cent of those who buy books do not read the books. But I still write. Why? It is only because I feel I must do so.

14

ATTENTION IS A PRECIOUS GIFT

Any man who can drive safely while kissing a pretty girl is simply not giving the kiss the attention it deserves.

—Albert Einstein

When I think back on my career, it seems to me that I spent the first two decades with more awareness about what my bosses and company owed me than about what I owed them in return. My experience is not unusual. I get the same result when I ask managers about the relative expectations from subordinate and boss. The list is always longer when it comes to the boss.

As I reflect on these last several months during which I have written these chapters, I cannot help feeling that the boss-subordinate relationship is like many other relationships. It is one of give and take, it is one of nurturing and managing, it is one in which neither party should take anything for granted.

It is one to which the gift of attention must be bestowed. Any relationship to which a person bestows attention is bound to succeed. Attention is the most precious gift a person can offer.

During my student days, I watched *Death of a Salesman,* a contemporary play by Pulitzer prize-winning writer Arthur Miller (see Box 14.1). I used to wonder why Willy Loman was so burnt-out that he killed himself. When I began my corporate career, I started to meet a real-life Willy Loman here, there and in many places. I desperately wanted to avoid repeating the sad experience of Willy Loman.

BOX 14.1: DEATH OF A SALESMAN

Willy Loman, a 60-year-old salesman, returns early from a business trip. After nearly crashing multiple times, Willy has a moment of enlightenment and realizes he shouldn't be driving. Seeing that her husband is no longer able to do his job as a travelling salesman, Willy's wife, Linda, suggests that he ask his boss, Howard, to give him a local office job at the New York headquarters. Willy thinks that getting the new job is a sure thing. But as things turn out, he had wrongly regarded himself as a valuable employee.

Willy and Linda's grown sons, Biff and Happy, are not particularly successful. Later that night, Willy starts having flashbacks and talks to imagined images as if they were real people. You guessed it. Something is wrong. Linda admits to her sons that she and Willy are struggling financially. Worse, Willy has been attempting suicide. She's worried and takes it out on her boys, accusing Biff of being the cause of Willy's

---

unhappiness. The next day, of course, everything goes wrong.

Willy feels happy and confident as he meets with his boss, Howard. But rather than give him a transfer to the New York office, Willy ends up getting fired. Destroyed by the news, he hallucinates, and once again starts to speak with imaginary people.

Unfortunately Willy can't get past his being a failure. He thinks the greatest contribution that he himself can make toward his sons' success is to commit suicide. That way, Biff could use the life insurance money to start a business. Within a few minutes, there's a loud bang. Willy has killed himself.

In the final scene, Linda, sobbing, still under the delusion that her husband was a well-liked salesman, wonders why no one came to his funeral.

Although the play was written many decades ago in 1949, it has had a revival in New York's Broadway. The *USA Today* correspondent quotes director Mike Nichols as saying, '*Death of a Salesman*, circa 2012, is very much about the here and now. Willy is still with us. There are many parallels to today. There is only so much to go around, as we are discovering. Everyone can't make it.'

WHY RELATIONSHIPS SUFFER AND BURN-OUTS HAPPEN

Considerable research on the subject has been done on the subject of burn-out by Prof Harry Levinson.[1] He has pointed out that burn-out symptoms include chronic fatigue, self-criticism, cynicism, negativity, anger and extreme display of emotions, all symptoms displayed by Willy Loman. Executive and organizational jobs involve intensive contact with people, including practical, working relationships with less capable colleagues and rivalry-driven, gossiping or self-centred people.

Work expectations appear less and less clear as you rise. What exactly am I supposed to deliver? How can I do so if I depend on so many others to cooperate? How can colleagues be allowed to block my actions without any obligation to advance my project? Why cannot the boss see what is so obvious and do something about it? Is it essential to create so much frustration among so many people?

Managing relationships is a stressful job, particularly as organizations inadvertently become unwieldy and opaque. The relationship with the CEO, whom you must read boss, is particularly crucial because it impacts your sense of self-esteem. Your self-esteem arises through the feeling of being valued and deriving the joy of fulfilment at work. In most cases when an employee does not enjoy going to work, the causes are traceable to the atmosphere in the workplace; in some way, the role of the departmental boss gets associated as one source of frustration.

In his paper, Levinson made a number of suggestions about how to prevent burn-out. I read those with a great deal of interest at the time when his paper was published. I tried to practise some of his suggestions and discovered some of my own.

Here are seven lessons from my experiences.

1. Keep physically fit because it is linked to emotional fitness

To deal with the stresses of work life, you have to be emotionally fit, and that requires you to be physically fit. It is no less important than physical fitness is for a top sportsman. This is elementary, but it is amazing how many executives ignore this aspect. Blood pressure, tension, stress, smoking and things like these are rampant in the management world. My friends and colleagues know how much I rely on my regime of sports and walking to retain my sanity. I can confirm that this has helped me to cope with the inevitable stresses of the workplace. The trouble is that many think that as you grow older, the ability to exercise decreases. That may be so but it is as you grow older that you need to keep the body parts moving; the fad for fitness must increase and that too, not through weekend gymnastics but through regular exercise.

2. Accept uncertainty and ambiguity as natural to the workplace

If you live in a big metropolis, you accept certain things as likely to be a part of your life: traffic snarls, pollution, crowds and noise, long commutes. You feel compensated for tolerating these shortcomings by aspects such as a vibrant commercial atmosphere, access to diverse customers, new job opportunities, better family facilities, and a rich repertoire of social events. The workplace of the future will be characterized by more uncertainties and ambiguities. There is only that much that your boss can do about reducing uncertainties because he himself is assailed by the same factors. Your sense of frustration and cynicism about the occurrence of uncertainties and contradictions can be mitigated by confronting the realities of the changing world.

3. Confront reality

Executives go through a phase when they just hope that problems will go away if they are left alone long enough. Papers may pile up in the in-tray or meetings on unpleasant subjects may not get scheduled. But usually, problems do not evaporate like rectified spirit. They hang around and get worse.

I am not advocating that you must act impetuously or rashly to demonstrate that you are confronting realities. I am merely advocating that you must act, learn from that action and repeat the cycle. The reality of both your life and career is that when you get into trouble, you have to get out yourself. I find the story of Italian mountaineer Walter Bonatti is particularly inspiring (see Box 14.2).

BOX 14.2: WALTER BONATTI

Walter Bonatti, who died in September 2011, was considered a pioneer in the area of technically difficult climbs. One of his most inspiring ones was recounted in the *New York Times* after his death. It is about the phenomenal escape that he devised when trapped by storms on the fifth day of his solo climb on the Petit Dru in the French Alps. There was no possibility of retreat. Bonatti attached a carabiner (a shaped ring with a spring catch on one side used for fastening ropes in mountaineering) to each of the three loops that he had tied in his rope and swung the rope up the cliff. Throw after throw, he persisted even when a carabiner that had snagged in an invisible crack 40 feet above popped loose at a slight tug, wrote Dave Roberts in the report. Finally, one carabiner held fast and he pulled himself up, hand over hand. It was 'probably the most important single climbing feat ever to take place in mountaineering', veteran climber Doug Scott was to call it.

4. You are paid to solve problems

It is because there are problems to be sorted out that you have a job in the first place. Problems in business do not come in neatly parcelled packages with a satin ribbon around them. They will be messy and difficult and the higher you are, the messier the problems will be. How can a tennis player feel hassled that the grass court is green or why should the cricketer feel that the ball is too hard? There are no problem-free jobs or bosses without hassles.

Most of us do learn to adapt to the hassles of the job and the boss. We do attend to solving the problem our company faces. It is when we fail to be adaptive that stresses begin and the boss relationship starts to fray. Competent managers tend to do their jobs effortlessly and without obvious stress in emotional terms.

5. Learn from your and others' mistakes

Executives are petrified of making mistakes because they are afraid of two things: what will their boss say and will it affect their career? This is not a misplaced concern.

However, the solution does not lie in mistake-avoidance, which may lead to possible inaction; rather it lies in minimizing the consequences of mistakes, taking small bets and learning from the experiences. Each day's work means that you are swimming in an ocean full of small mistakes by you and by others. Each mistake teaches you a lesson. That is how you learn from adversity.

Stanford academic Carol Dweck is a leading expert on why some people are better at learning from mistakes and some others are not. Her view is that though all of us have a combination of a fixed mindset (= your abilities are fixed and success comes out of repeatedly using the same abilities) and a growth mindset (=your abilities can change if you learn from mistakes and are willing to put in the effort), each of us tends to lean towards one or the other, depending on the context in which we find ourselves.

According to Dweck, basketball star Michael Jordan has a growth mindset. He is fiercely competitive, and irrespective of whether he wins or loses, he is honest with himself. He blames nobody and constantly tries to improve his own capabilities. On the other hand, tennis star John McEnroe has a fixed mindset. He used to be notorious for his tantrums and when he started to lose, he blamed everybody and everything for his problems, but not himself.

The psychology department of the University of Pennsylvania provides a small dialogue about making mistakes and learning.

Q: What is the secret of your success?
A: Two words.

Q: What are they?
A: Right decisions.

Q: How do you make right decisions?
A: One word.

Q: What is that?
A: Experience.

Q: How do you get experience?
A: Two words

Q: What are they?
A: Wrong decisions.

6. Develop the capacity to bounce back after near-death

No one wants to deliberately court near-death situations. They occur on their own. When they do, your experience of getting out of the situation teaches you a lot about who you really are.

Bipin Shah, my boss, had the job of turning around a sick dairy in Etah, UP in 1973; I was assisting him and, by God, it felt like a near-death situation: we were caught between a hard rock and a stone. HLL had tried to close the plant but the chief minister persuaded the chairman not to do so, 'If HLL cannot run it profitably, nobody can. Please save the jobs and try.' Bipin Shah taught me the art of entering a maze of business problems, doing some corrections, and emerging to study the results—and then go in again.

It is a bit like what the Cisco chairman, John Chambers, recounts about his company, 'We're a product of the challenges we faced and how we handled those challenges. In 2001, we went from being the most valuable company in the world to a company where they questioned whether the leadership was really effective.'[2]

Academic Karl Weicz has written about Organization and Strategy and he has quoted a fascinating story about a Hungarian lieutenant. The source is an anecdote related by Albert Szent-Gyorgyi (1893-1986), probably to Miroslav Holub or to people he knew, some time before 1977. The incident from which it stems seems to have occurred during the Second World War. Holub recorded it as a poem (see Box 14.3).

BOX 14.3: THE LOST CONTINGENT

The *Poem on the Hungarian Lieutenant* narrates the trauma of Albert Szent-Gyorgyi, a young lieutenant of a small Hungarian detachment in the Alps, when the reconnaissance unit that he had sent out into the frosty wasteland did not return for two days. He bemoaned that he had sent his own people to an icy grave. On day three, the unit returned and claimed that when they thought that all was lost, somebody found a map in his pocket. This calmed them. They waited for the storm to abate, found their bearings and were back!

The lieutenant took a good look at the map. 'It was not a map of the Alps / but of the Pyrenees', he found.

The message of the incident in management terms is: 'The value of a map, just like the value of a strategic framework, model or image, comes not from its ability to represent the environment objectively in all its detail, but from its ability to focus minds and help people take a particular course.'[3]

7. Enjoy what you do and do what you enjoy

I have found that if the work that you do is at the core of who you are, there is less chance of burn-out. That is perhaps why I have not found it stressful to teach students or to write this book, though these are strenuous amidst a busy professional life.

Observe how world-class sportsmen, artists, musicians and corporate executives seem to do their work with seeming effortlessness. You realize their feat only when you try to emulate it. In fact they seem to have no work-life balance issues because their work is their life and their life is their work.

This does not mean that all of us should merge our work and personal life. Anyway most of us are not world-class. We must respect our families and never compromise on domestic duties and raising our kids. The kids will never be kids again. The value of happy relationships in life and a stable family cannot be underestimated.

Such things may not normally require to be proved, but thanks to academics, there is proof for what your common sense tells you. There has been a Grant Study to prove that happiness comes out of good health and warm relationships[4] (see Box 14.4).

BOX 14.4: WHAT MAKES US HAPPY?

The Grant Study followed the lives of 240 men in the Harvard class of 1937.

It began with full physical and psychological evaluations of all the young men, and for seventy-three years it followed their progress in all areas of their life—physical, social, emotional, and professional.

This study was the longest quality of life research project ever conducted, and it was presided over since the 1960's by psychologist Dr George Vaillant. Some of its findings were analysed in an article in *Atlantic Magazine*.[4]

The study traced the stories of these men's lives. Some showed unbelievable changes. Many students who started off brilliantly fizzled out and developed problems; many students who began with problems worked through them and died happy old men.

There are several key insights from the study, which identified key variables in happiness:

a. education
b. stable marriage
c. not smoking
d. not abusing alcohol
e. some exercise and healthy weight, and
f. to develop healthy adaptation.

The predictive power of these factors is high.

You know these even without research. So practise what you know.

REFERENCES

2. Adapt through the Journey

1. *Why Smart People Do Stupid Things,* Gene F. Ostrom, iUniverse Inc, 2008
2. *Emotional Intelligence,* Daniel Goleman, Bantam Books, 1995
3. *Social Intelligence,* Daniel Goleman, Bantam Books, 2006
4. *The Great Intimidators,* Roderick M. Kramer, *Harvard Business Review,* February 2006
5. *Jack Welch and Work-Life Balance,* Eric Sorensen, CNBC, 27 July 2009
6. *Five Minds for the Future,* Howard Gardner, Harvard Business School Press, 2006

3. The 4 As: The Attributes of the High Potential Manager

1. *Quiet: The Power of Introverts in a World That Can't Stop Talking,* Susan Cain, Viking, 2010
2. *Execution: The Discipline of Getting Things Done,* Larry Bossidy and Ram Charan, Crown Business, 2002
3. *The Knowing-Doing Gap: How Smart Companies Turn Knowledge into Action,* Jeffrey Pfeffer and Robert Sutton, Harvard Business School Press, 1999
4. *When the Penny Drops,* R. Gopalakrishnan, Penguin India, 2010
5. 'Lessons of Silence,' Bruno Kahne, *Strategy + Business,* 22 May 2008

6. *Trust: The One Thing That Makes or Breaks a Leader,* Les T. Csorba, Pearson Power, 2004

4. Deliver Results Reliably

1. *Living Well,* Mihaly Csikszentmihaly, Weidenfeld and Nicholson, 1997
2. *When the Penny Drops,* R. Gopalakrishnan, Penguin India, 2010
3. 'Inside Pfizer's Palace Coup,' Peter Elkind and Jennifer Reingold, *Fortune Asia Pacific,* 15 August 2011
4. *The Difficulty of Being Good,* Gurcharan Das, Allen Lane, 2009

5. Offer Solutions

1. 'Recognizing Creative Leadership: Can Creative Idea Expression Negatively Relate to Perceptions of Leadership Potential?' Jennifer Mueller, Jack Goncalo, and Dishan Kamdar, *Journal of Experimental Psychology,* December 2010
2. 'Managing Your Boss,' John J. Gabarro and John P. Kotter, *Harvard Business Review,* January 2005

6. Bring Dynamism to Work

1. *When You Say Yes but Mean No,* Leslie Perlow, Crown Business, 2003

7. How to Balance Self-Interest with the Company's Interest

1. *The TCS Story,* S. Ramadorai, Penguin India, 2011
2. *The Cost of Bad Behaviour,* Christine Pearson and Christine Porath, Portfolio, 2009
3. 'Managing with the Brain in Mind,' David Rock, *Strategy + Business,* Autumn 2009
4. *Ideas That Have Worked,* Viking, 2004

10. Communicate and Carry Co-workers

1. *Taking People with You*, David Novak, Portfolio Penguin, 2012.
2. 'Using Stories to Persuade,' John Baldoni, HBR.org http://blogs.hbr.org/cs/2011/03/using_stories_as_a_tool_of_per.html
3. *The Case of the Bonsai Manager*, R. Gopalakrishnan, Penguin India, 2007

11. Interact with and Carry All Stakeholders

1. *The Science of Success*, Charles G. Koch, John Wiley, 2007

12. The Dilemmas of Authenticity

1. 'Managing Authenticity: The Paradox of Great Leadership,' Rob Goffee and Gareth Jones, *Harvard Business Review*, December 2005
2. *A CEO's Moral Stand*, Michael Lindsay, *New York Times*, 30 November 2011

13. Remember Who You Are

1. *Remember Who You Are: Life Stories That Inspire the Heart and Mind*, Daisy Wademan, Harvard Business School Press, 2004.

14. Attention Is a Precious Gift

1. 'When Executives Burn Out,' Harry Levinson, *Harvard Business Review*, May/June 1981.
2. *Bouncing Back Is What Sets a Leader Apart*, Adam Bryant, *International Herald Tribune*, 3 August, 2009
3. *Images of Strategy*, Stephen Cummings and David Wilson, Blackwell Publishing.
4. *What Makes Us Happy*, Joshua Wolf Shenk, *Atlantic Magazine*, June 2009

INDEX

ABOUT THE AUTHOR

R. Gopalakrishnan (Gopal to his friends) brings his rich management experience to this book. He has worked in international and Indian companies, has lived in India and abroad, and has developed a global perspective about business and people.

Gopal has worked for forty-five years as a professional manager from 1967 onwards: thirty-one in Unilever and fourteen in Tata. Currently he is Director, Tata Sons Limited. He had served Unilever as Chairman of Unilever Arabia, as Managing Director of Brooke Bond Lipton India, and as Vice-Chairman of Hindustan Lever Limited. Gopal studied physics at St. Xavier's Calcutta, engineering at IIT Kharagpur, and also attended the Advanced Management Program at Harvard Business School.

He has earlier authored The Case of the Bonsai Manager: *Lessons for Managers on Intuition* (2007) and When the Penny Drops: *Learning What Is Not Taught* (2010).

He has delivered guest lectures in India and abroad and his articles have been published widely. He has taught a credit course entitled LWNT: Learning What's Not Taught at leading management institutions. He is a past president of the All-India Management Association.